Lake Mind

ISBN: 1-4196-6976-1
ISBN-13: 978-1419669767

CHARLES E. MULLIS SR.

LAKE MIND
A FRESH LOOK AT SANCTIFICATION

2008

Lake Mind

"Not your every Sunday morning conversation"

I turned in for the evening and made up my mind what I was going to do about this 'Christianity stuff'. I was 19 years old, a newlywed and miserable. The turmoil boiling constantly on the inside of me had taken its toll and I had to have some relief.

I woke up early the next morning and got ready for work. As I was tying my work boots my wife stirred and with a confused look asked, "What are you doing?"

"I'm going to work." I replied as I finished tying my shoes.

Even more bewildered she responded with, "But Charles, it's Sunday." I had been sitting on the edge of our bed tying my shoes and this conversation was taking place without me looking at her.

I lowered my head and quietly yet with determination I said, "I know it's Sunday and I don't care." Then turning and looking at her I explained, "I'm sorry. I can't do this Christian thing. It doesn't work for me. I don't care if you continue to go to church and you can tithe our income if you want, but I'm through!"

By now she was beside herself and asked in a pleading voice, "What am I going to tell them at church?"

"Tell them to go to hell!" I replied and added, "And tell them not to come here to visit me. I'm through with church!" With that said I walked out and went to work.

"How I got into this condition"

Shortly before my eighteenth birthday I heard and committed to the gospel of salvation in a Baptist church. Prior to that, my church attendance was limited to family funerals and weddings. My dad was a self-employed trim carpenter who worked seven days a week while I was growing up and, when my two brothers and I were not in school, we were working with him. So I grew up on construction sites around some of the roughest and rowdiest men you can imagine. By the time I was a teenager I knew more about the world of alcohol, pornography, dirty jokes, and cheating on women than most grown men ever will.

When I heard the gospel I was ecstatic with the reality of forgiveness. The only problem was that I kept crawling back to my early training. At first the newness of my experience enabled me to resist temptations, but before long I found myself slipping into my old habits, which began what seemed like an cycle of sinning and repenting; walking the aisle at church only to slip up and go back on my commitment to the Lord.

That morning when I went to work instead of to church I was walking away from a class I was teaching as well as the post of church training director. I told the Lord that night that I was sorry for letting Him down and that I had really tried but it was useless for me to continue. Evidently I wasn't cut out to be a Christian and I told Him I wouldn't do any more damage to His kingdom by being such a poor excuse of a disciple. I told Him to leave me alone! He didn't listen! Now—34 years later—I am so glad He didn't.

"My problem stemmed from not understanding the cost of sanctification."

The standard teaching in my church amounted to nothing less than a misconception about sanctification. The concept that was sold to me and many others goes like this:

1) Stay busy with religious activity and eventually you will outgrow your sinful past;

2) Never admit to the personal struggles you are experiencing because it may discourage others from trying Christianity;
3) Bible study, prayer, tithing, and going on visitation are all you need to do to be a good Christian.

On the outside I was a 'good church member' but on the inside I was one sorry follower of Christ—and the struggle within was killing me. In the back of my mind I kept hearing my dad say as he would teach me about being a carpenter, "Son, anything worth doing is worth doing right." Which would be followed by, "And if you can't do it right don't do it at all." So, after a couple of years of feeling like I had given it my best shot, I walked away.

My wife was totally confused mainly because she knew nothing of my struggle. It would be years later before I even knew myself the real nature of the problem. Now, in defense of my pastor and fellow church members, they informed me that I needed to experience the 'process of sanctification'. They also led me to believe that I was doing all that was necessary by being involved in church. I discovered however, that this 'status quo' level of Christianity was really nothing more than 'churchianity'. I realize that churchianity is not a word, but it best describes what I was indoctrinated with.

I was an exceptional church member. When the doors were open, I was there. It didn't take long before I had my own key and was there even more. The point, however, is that it wasn't the right process or system to enable me to overcome my past. Had I not walked out—had I stayed in the system as it had been sold to me—I would still be as miserable and messed up today. Instead, my abandonment of Christianity only lasted about three months.

That Sunday on my way home I stopped and bought a six pack of beer and a certain familiar magazine. I don't know why, because when I got home I put the beer in the refrigerator and threw the magazine onto the top shelf of my closet, touching neither for three months. What had tormented me from my past was not even appealing enough for me to do anything with other than buy it.

Then one Wednesday after Cathy had gone to church, I defiantly determined to exercise my right to drink beer and read pornographic material. So I went to the fridge, took out what used to be my favorite beer, took a taste…and poured it into the sink. The next five followed. I then retrieved the magazine and threw it in the trash without even opening it to the first page.

After that, I went outside and sat on the edge of my front porch and began to think. Somewhere in the process of thinking about my miserable existence scriptures began to come to mind and the Spirit of God began to work.

By the time I got up from that seat on the porch I had two scriptures prominent in my thinking. They were Romans 8:28 and Hebrews 11:6.

"For we know that God causes all things to work together for good to those who are the called according to His purpose" Rom. 8:28a NASB

"But without faith it is impossible to please Him, for He who comes to Him must believe that He is, and that He is a rewarder of those who diligently seek Him." Heb. 11:6 NKJV

Before I got up from that seat I had received an assurance from the Spirit of God, through the Word of God, that He would change me and then use me to help others. I went back to church the following Sunday and apologized to the congregation and sought their help. They did not disappoint me, but only because I was not depending on them but rather on the Lord.

Things at the church had not changed—I had. It didn't take very long for me to realize that 'church as usual' was not going to work for me. Nor will it work for any one else with a past to overcome. I pointed myself toward God and when things went wrong I just kept going toward Him. I decided that He was going to change me in spite of my failures because I had assurance from His Word that He was working in all things to bring about good, so I sought Him regardless of my circumstances.

What I have written in these pages is the gleaning of what the Spirit taught me as He renewed my mind with the Word. Before you go any further know this...The cost of sanctification is *'everything'*. Are you willing to pay the price? Reading this work and following the prescribed process will cost you. It will cost you the loss of the misery you live with in your mind and will pay you with the dividends of peace, trust, and reliance on a God who paid everything to make you His.

SECTION ONE
LAKE MIND—A USEFUL METAPHOR

CHAPTER ONE
A SIMPLE ILLUSTRATION IS BORN

When I look back at my earliest memories of hearing testimonies it seems that they all had one thing in common; they were superficial to the point of being fictional. Actually I don't really believe they were completely fictional. Usually there were enough facts to make them sound believable. Most of the time these testimonies were given by men and I soon discovered that I could look at the wife while the man was speaking and get a pretty good idea as to the validity of what was being professed.

We have all heard testimonies of how, after tithing, miraculous figures appeared in a checkbook, or how someone came to Christ and they quit drinking and haven't even wanted a taste since. It's not that I don't think such things are possible, it's just that I find them hard to believe.

I am somewhat a *mystic* when it comes to my prayer life. I'm not a charismatic who experiences manifestations and I don't hear a distinct voice in my head that I consider to be divine in origin. Nonetheless, I do pray and seek answers. I believe in communing with the Almighty by praying and listening. It's just that I accept what the writer of the letter to the Hebrews said in 1:1, "*God, who at various times and in various ways spoke in time past to the fathers by the prophets, has in these last days spoken to us by His Son*". What God has to say He has said through the life of Jesus Christ who is described in the gospel of John as "the Word of God". We have recorded in the New Testament a reference for every situation we will ever encounter.

When I hear from God I am hearing from the Word. He will never lead me by any other means nor in any way that contradicts what He has said in His Word. He is not excluded from working in my circumstances outside conventional means, but He will not violate that which He has already laid down for us in the Word. Nor is He limited to that which I am able to understand. After all, He is God! The problem most of us have with God is that He acts like He is God! As a friend of mine says, "God is sovereign and that means He's in charge!"

God has laid out in His Word what we call the process of sanctification. When we use the term 'process' we distinguish between the instantaneous setting apart that happens at the moment of regeneration and faith. Shortly after I became a Christian I was taught how as believers our salvation is done in three phases:

First, I am saved from the penalty of sin and, though I will continue to wrestle with it, I am no longer condemned to hell. Second, I am being saved each day from the power of sin. And third, I will be saved from the presence of sin when I enter into heaven.

It is the 'being saved' that we are examining here and, while it will exclude a lot of PowerPoint testimonies like I was hearing in my youth, it will include power-filled results of lives transformed by the Word of God.

"A Confused Look Results in the Illustration of Lake Mind"

In the introduction, I shared a glimpse of my Christian beginnings. Now let's move forward about ten years to a point where I had overcome a significant amount of the perverse training I received as a youngster and had become a respected teacher and counselor in a large suburban church.

Each Sunday I taught the Sanctuary Bible Class at our church. As a conference speaker I conducted numerous seminars and workshops on subjects of marriage, prayer, finances, and spiritual warfare. These activities resulted in a significant number of requests for counseling. So, for about 6-8 hours each week I was in my church office holding private sessions with those in need. It was during this time that I met Gayle

Gayle was a single mom in her mid forties who had not been to church since childhood. Her life was already filled with difficulties and now she had the added problem of having been diagnosed with cancer. She came to me because her sister had attended a class I gave on spiritual warfare in which I shared the experience of fasting and praying for over a year concerning my son's struggle with epilepsy. This sister knew that there were more things wrong in Gayle's life than cancer. She had recently led Gayle to a saving knowledge of Christ and Gayle was struggling significantly in her new found faith. Not long after her conversion she learned she had cancer.

Our first conversation went something like this:

Charles: How can I help you today?

Gayle: I have cancer, I am dying and my sister says you can help me. I went to my pastor and he talked to me to be sure I was saved and told me to get ready to die. But I just can't handle it. Will you help me get ready to die?

Charles: Do you want to die?

Gayle: No, but I've got cancer and the doctors have given me six to eight weeks to live.

Charles: Gayle, if you don't want to die I can't help you. You don't know for sure that it's God's will for you to die from this cancer. Now if you want me to help you to live until you die I can help you with that.

Gayle: What do you mean?

Charles: Let me put it to you this way. Do you know when

I would accept that it was God's will for me to die from this cancer?

Gayle: When?

Charles: About 10 seconds after I died—and at that point I would no longer care. Until I died, though, I would spend my time praying for healing.

Gayle: How can I know if he will heal me?

Charles: 10 seconds after you die you'll know He didn't heal you. And at that point you will understand and won't care. Until then I would look toward healing, not toward death. Do you understand?

Gayle: Yes, let's get started.

At that point I began to ask about her background. At first she resisted opening up about her past, but after I shared with her the testimony of my son's healing from epilepsy she saw the reasoning behind confronting her past.

Gayle (just like you and I) was not a neutral, amoral creature who was attacked one day by a deadly disease. She was a composite of her ancestry coupled with all her life's experiences. Very little that transpires in any of our lives comes about arbitrarily.

I am not saying that all illnesses are related to our history. Jesus was asked about a blind man who was born without sight. His disciples wanted to know who sinned and caused it, him or his parents. Jesus informed them that it was neither. Rather this man's infirmity was for the glory of God at that very moment. Jesus healed the man and God was glorified.

However, a significant proportion of the difficulties we face in life are direct consequences of our actions and I am not just limiting these actions to the category of sin. The fall affected all of creation and the consequences have been passed on to us, but most of the difficulties I have seen and experienced have been related to personal failures.

Therefore, in order to gain a better understanding of what I am dealing with I begin each session by getting a brief history from those who come for help. If the problem is finances we investigate spending habits and financial history. This investigation may lead us to discover problems that, on the surface, seem unrelated.

Most the problems we have are related to something in our past that we no longer can or want to recall. Remembering is not our problem. We never forget anything. It is the inability or refusal to recall memories that plague us.

I had developed a fairly competent ability to ask the right questions during counseling. Gayle provided a challenge that would result in a simple illustration that has helped thousands and I hope will help many more through this book.

Gayle was a very intelligent woman, but did not see any reason to study certain scriptures if they had nothing to do with healing or cancer. Finally about our third session she admitted that she was not doing what I asked her to in the way of study and prayer. I had taken her to passages numerous times that related to the power of God's Word and she felt that she didn't have the time to waste learning scripture. I knew if I could make her see the importance of the Word flowing through her mind she would do it. So right there in our third session we both watched 'lake mind' unfold.

Perhaps the single greatest common interest my wife and I have is fresh water fishing. While dating and then in the early years of our life together we spent most of our recreational time fishing a brackish creek that feeds the St. Johns River in Jacksonville. This water had a very dark texture and even its shallowest areas offered excellent fishing. This changed however over a period of several years.

In the early 1970's several anti-pollution laws caused the paper mills and power plants to clean up their use of the air and water in our town. Consequently as the years passed and the water cleared, the spots that seemed always to produce good fishing action now were abandoned. The reason? The water was so clear the fish could see us and flee the area before we could cast our lures. Before they were attacking movement and the appearance of bait; now they swim away, no longer being fooled.

This is what created the understanding of the sanctification process…"being saved". One of the reasons I stopped fishing in that creek was because of how clear it had become, making most of the formerly productive spots not worth the effort.

I realized that the process of sanctification is a lot like fishing in that brackish creek. You know the root of the problem is somewhere in the dark water of your memory. The question then is, "How do we discover what is in the past that is messing up the present and ruining the future?"

Shortly after Gayle and I began our session I felt totally frustrated and helpless. In front of me sat a woman who had only weeks to live and I wanted to help her but could not seem to impress on her the need to open her mind to the Word and then the Spirit of God. Earlier I mentioned that I am somewhat of a mystic and I sought to give the understanding that any mysticism that I might experience is limited to the Word of God and guided by the Holy Spirit. I would now like to further develop that thought.

First of all, seeking answers from the spiritual realm opens one up to the possibility of response from any spirit. Depending on your ancestry, background, and present involvement you might receive an idea that does not have its origin in the divine.

Second, the only way to be sure that the answers you receive in prayer are from the Lord is to check them against His Word. If an answer violates any principle found in scripture it is a sure sign that it is not God's answer. However, the ability to utilize this check and balance between request and response is limited by your understanding of the principles found in the Word.

Therefore my method in counseling is to discover where a person is violating, or has violated in the past, the principle of scripture, show him or her where their actions are in violation, and how the circumstances they are in are a result of it. Gayle understood my words but did not grasp the concept.

Now I don't believe that every adverse circumstance that happens upon us is the result of sin or disobedience. As already stated, some are for the glory of God and we may never gain an understanding of them this side of heaven. However, if only a percentage of them are related to our own actions it is worth the time and effort to sort things out.

That is what I was attempting with Gayle. With only weeks available I needed to sort out if there was anything in her life that might be causing this illness. The clock literally was ticking and it would be an understatement to tell you I was concerned. So out of frustration I stopped and said, "Let's pray."

I begin every session with prayer and often pray about things we might be dealing with as the session goes forward, so this interruption was not unusual. It was however one of those exceptional times when I sensed the Spirit praying through me. All the information coming together was already in my mind, but the way it was put together was not my doing. Without saying 'amen' I asked Gayle to open her eyes while I pulled out a blank sheet of paper and began to show her what I had visualized as I prayed.

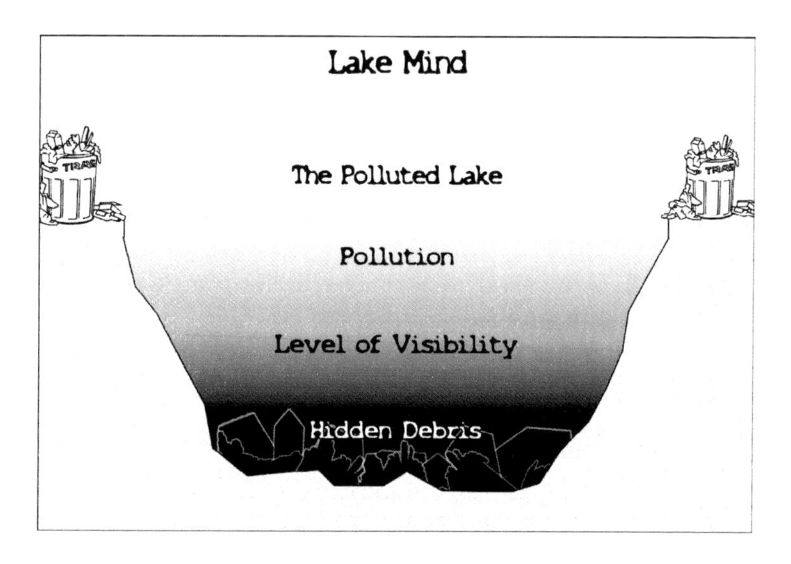

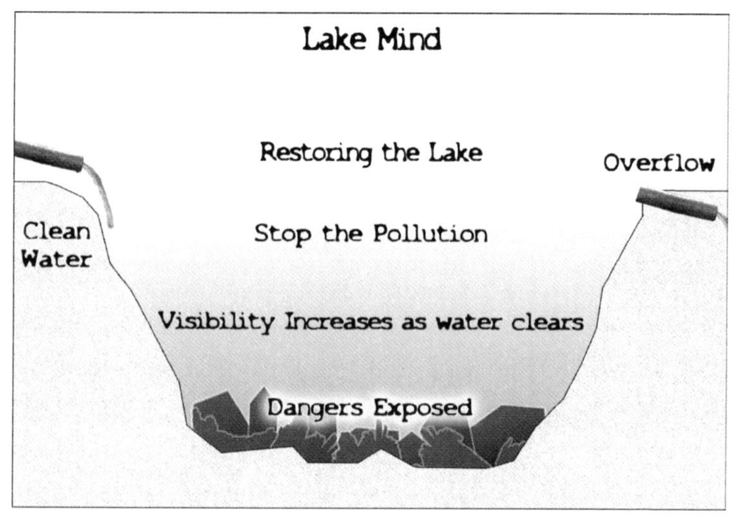

I said, "Imagine for a moment that we are standing on the edge of a lake that is surrounded by all sorts of garbage and trash. We can see the perimeter of this lake is polluted, but can only imagine what's under the surface of the water." Gayle looked at me as if I were insane. I looked at her and asked, "Do you trust me?" She nodded her head, so I said, "Hear me out then."

"You and I decide that we want to become more socially responsible and reclaim this lake and restore it to its natural beauty. The first thing we have got to do is to stop any more pollution from getting into it. After all, it will be useless to deal with this trash if we allow the pollution process to continue. So we are going to put up a fence and post a guard to ensure that no one can come along and add to the pollution.

Once we have prevented the pollution from getting worse, we can begin to clean up all the visible garbage and begin to think about what's there that we cannot see. Cleaning up surface debris is work and will take time, so while we are engaged in that task we are going to start a process that will help us to deal with anything that is hidden below the surface. The process we are going to engage in will change the texture of the water in the lake from dark and obscure to clear and transparent. That way we will be able to remove the trash that is below the surface.

Are you with me so far?" She nodded, so I continued.

While I was talking, I had been drawing a simple illustration of the lake, its water, the trash, and the fence. I pointed to the drawing and noted out how the pollution allowed us to only see a few inches into the depth of the lake, then began to speculate about the dangers lurking below in the unknown.

Then I drew a water spout on one side to indicate a continuous stream of water pouring into the lake and said, "What we are going to do is displace the polluted water with clean water. So here we are providing a fresh and uncontaminated source that, over time, will displace the old with the new. I must warn you, however, that as this new water pours in it will stir up a lot of junk that had settled to the bottom, so things may initially appear worse. But don't worry; the good will overcome the bad.

Next, on the opposite side of the lake from the water spout, I drew an overflow outlet. If we do not have an outlet we may have even more problems as the water level rises and overflows its banks.

As time passes and the clean water displaces the polluted water, we start to see deeper into the lake. We can now see that there are objects that should not be in our lake and we can safely remove them. As the water continues to clear and we see deeper below the surface, larger or more substantial objects are revealed. Some of them are so substantial that we may have to get help to remove them or even leave some of them. If leaving them is the best course of action at least we are aware of them and can avoid them.

At that point I looked at Gayle and said, "Gayle, the name of our lake is Lake Mind. This drawing illustrates what I have been trying to get you to do with the scriptures and prayers over the last couple of weeks. The passages I have wanted you to study will help us find out if there is anything in your past that may be the cause of your physical problems."

Once Gayle understood the rationale for the process, it began to work. After additional time together we had discovered and confessed some detrimental events from her past. At our last session I took her to James 5, where our Lord's half-brother gives us instructions for praying for those who are sick, and I instructed her to go back to her pastor and request prayer. I warned her that not many churches practiced the instruction in James 5 and told her to demand, if necessary, that the church pray for her.

Less than a week later, Gayle came in for an appointment. I could tell by the smile on her face that she had good news. She had done as instructed and her pastor called the deacons forward at the end of the Wednesday evening service. The church laid hands on her and prayed for healing. The very next day she was scheduled to go back for more cancer treatment. The doctor ran a series of tests to see if the chemo was working. Remarkably—dare I say miraculously?—The cancer was not in remission; it simply was not there!

For the sake of time this entire event has been condensed somewhat, but I promise you is accurate. Gayle shared her testimony everywhere she went and became a leader in her church singles department until she died 17 years later from heart disease.

Now that I've explained the concept of Lake Mind to you, let's draw a parallel between Lake Mind and Sanctification, what we term "being saved". But first, allow me to provide this disclaimer. I might seem to be making a big deal out of this simple illustration, but really I am not. I didn't even think anything of it for some time. Then, while teaching at a seminar, I began to get the same confused looks from my audience as I was trying to explain the process of being transformed, so without planning to I jumped in with the illustration. This was a rather large group at a retreat center and the introduction of this simple illustration created quite a stir.

I taught it together with the Timeline of Development (which follows later). Throughout the weekend participants would come up to me and draw the lake in the air and ask questions or make confirming comments. I knew from the first such encounter that Lake Mind would be an effective tool for understanding sanctification.

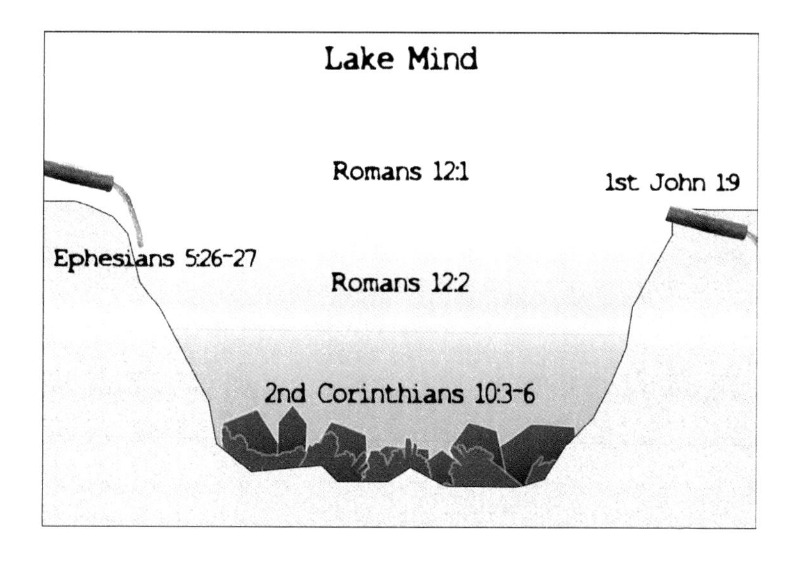
Lake Mind
Romans 12:1
1st John 1:9
Ephesians 5:26-27
Romans 12:2
2nd Corinthians 10:3-6

CHAPTER TWO
THE LAKE AS METAPHOR

We now will examine the process of sanctification as it relates to the illustration.

Step 1

"Stop the Pollution"

Once we made the decision to restore the lake, the first order of business was to stop the pollution process. Romans 12:1-2 says, " *I beseech you therefore, brethren, by the mercies of God that you present your bodies a living sacrifice, holy, acceptable to God, which is your reasonable service. And do not be conformed to this world, but be transformed by the renewing of your mind, that you may prove what is that good and acceptable and perfect will of God."*

This passage is the scripture behind the decision to reclaim the lake and stop the pollution. Let's break down this process. The first step in reclaiming our dysfunctional lives is the 'recognition of ownership'. Paul extols us to 'give our bodies as a living sacrifice' and it is to be done based on the 'mercies of God' that have been shown previously in his letter. Therefore the method of sacrifice is through, 'stopping our conformity to this world'. Inherent within the language is the idea of stopping something that is ongoing.

Paul's pleading is based on the fact that God in His mercy has redeemed us through the sacrifice of His Son and that redemption establishes His ownership of our total being. Therefore, our sacrifice has become a 'reasonable act of service'.

The second part of stopping our conformity to this world is the process of renewing our mind. We must be 'transformed' from our worldly way of thinking over to God's way of thinking.

Another thought that may have been in Paul's command that we give our bodies as sacrifice might be found in his description of the struggle we have with the flesh found in chapter 7. *"I find then a law, that evil is present with me, the one who wills to do good. For I delight in the law of God according to the inward man. But I see another law in my members, warring against the law of my mind, and bringing me into captivity to the law of sin which is in my members. O wretched man that I am! Who will deliver me from this body of death? I thank God, through Jesus Christ our Lord! So then, with the mind I myself serve the law of God, but with the flesh the law of sin." 21-25*

This law of the flesh is the inborn spirit of rebellion that we inherited from the father of mankind, Adam. Couple this spirit of rebellion with the curse of the fall and multiply it by the generations that have passed and you have the modern mindset.

"Syncretism: The Order of the Day"

If you were to ask me what the largest impediment to the church today is in both the universal body and the local assembly I would not hesitate to answer 'syncretism'. Syncretism is the marriage of opposing belief systems into a unified practice. The best biblical example is found in I Kings 17&18 where Elijah does battle with the prophets of Baal. In this decisive story, Elijah calls for a drought for 3½ years because of Israel's embracing of Jezebel and her false religion of Baal worship. Just prior to the end of the drought, Elijah calls for a showdown between the God of Judaism and the Baal god. The story ends with Elijah in victory, the prophets of Baal dead, and the people turning back to the true worship of God—at least for a while.

The problem that brought about this confrontation was not Israel's abandonment of the worship of Jehovah and the temple sacrifices, but rather the addition of Baal worship to the ritual of Judaism. The people did not abandon their service to God; they just added service to Baal. Baal worship consisted of heterosexual and homosexual involvement with the priests and priestesses of Baal in booths set up outside the temple. They believed that this activity allowed the Baal god to overcome the goddess of the Mediterranean Sea, rape her, and then move from the ocean to the mountain tops where, with fire and rain, he fertilized the crops and blessed his worshipers. By embracing Baal, the people of God were scratching their sensual itches and at the same time supposedly assuring themselves of a healthy harvest as if to be saying, "Jehovah has His part and Baal has the other". This blend of belief systems was in violation of their covenant with God and brought about His judgment.

Today, the syncretism that is crippling the church is the marriage of theism and humanism. Theism proclaims that God is the measure while humanism touts that man is the measure. I remember as a young believer wondering what all the fuss was about concerning a woman's right to get an abortion. "After all," I reasoned, "it was just a fetus." I'm sorry to say that my attitude was not unique in the church at that time, nor is it today.

The only way to overturn this humanistic infiltration of Christianity is by individually giving our bodies sacrificially so we can begin the process of renewing our minds. This is the philosophical mindset for stopping the pollution. The practical application requires doing whatever it takes to stop filling our minds with our own self-gratification. To do that, we must stop the trash from going into our mind. I hate get on this particular soapbox, but there is very little in the entertainment industry that is not humanistic in both philosophy and practice. I am not saying that we should all trash our TV's and never go to a movie, but we must practice discernment, especially if what we are viewing feeds our humanity to the point that it erodes our faith. Ask yourself, "Who does this serve? And what purpose does it fulfill?" You cannot serve two masters. If you are going to renew your mind you need to stop allowing just any old thing to come into it. You have got to consecrate your mind and give it over to the influence of God's Spirit.

In the Lake Mind illustration I described the necessity of putting up whatever barriers are necessary to stop the pollution. When we are talking about our minds, these barriers are not easy to define, let alone put in place. The things that have polluted our minds have found their entrance through our five senses: sight, touch, taste, feel, and smell. These senses are the doorway to our thoughts and are always at work.

"Tackle your problems one at a time."

Let's take the advice of the writer of the letter to the Hebrews. In chapter twelve he challenges the believers to run the race set before them and to *"lay aside the sin that so easily besets them."* Note that his encouragement is to deal with that which is hindering forward progress. If you are like I was, you can't count all the sins that are tripping you up. Nor can you clean house completely before you move forward. Just identify one thing that pollutes your mind the most and set up a barrier and move on to the next step. For example let's say sexual lust is your main point of weakness. You might do some of the following:

- Stay away from movies, art, or anything visual that puts suggestive pictures in your mind.
- Don't read suggestive material.
- If a billboard on the way to work causes a problem, pick a new route.
- Stop taking the second glance (we can't always stop what pops up in front of us, but we can refuse to continue to look).

As a young married man I found that I could not think impure thoughts of anyone and think of my wife at the same time. When I discovered this and began trying it I was so stirred by thoughts of my wife that I left my job and went to a pay phone and called her. She was surprised to say the least and wanted to know what I had done (as if a fellow can't call his wife because he is thinking of her). I assured her that it was just because I was thinking of her and she suspiciously accepted my answer. As you can imagine, in my early battles with sexual lust I called my wife often. On construction sites I found that I had to refuse to read the walls of the portable restrooms. All of these things required that I make a choice. And that's what you will need to do if you are serious about overcoming these temptations. You have to keep choosing what is beneficial. No matter how often you need to do it, keep choosing what is honorable and right and beneficial. Only when you stop making that choice will you fail.

We will deal more with this in detail later, for now let's move to the next step.

If thoughts of lust occupy your thinking you will primarily be battling memories that are visual in nature. However, the smell of a certain perfume might also stimulate those thoughts.

Hearing someone's voice may jar a memory that starts lustful thoughts.

Someone once said:

Sow a thought, reap an action,

Sow an action, reap a habit,

Sow a habit, reap character

If we accept this progression as true, then it is incumbent on us to begin the process of changing our thoughts if we are to change our habits and then our character. We do not exist in a vacuum and our mind abhors one. You will never change your life simply by stopping an activity. You must displace that which you would change. If you take something out, you must put something else in.

Listen to the charge Paul gives to the Christians at Ephesus in 4:17-28. "*So I tell you this, and insist on it in the Lord, that you must no longer live as the gentiles do, in the futility of their thinking. They are darkened in their understanding and separated from the life of God because of the ignorance that is in them due to the hardening of their hearts. Therefore each of you must put off falsehood and speak truthfully to his neighbor, he who has been stealing must steal no longer, but must work, doing something useful with his hands in order that he may have something to give to those in need.*"

We are not to engage in *futile thinking.* Notice the activities that they are to follow: "Don't lie, speak the truth; don't steal, go to work and have something to give"

The reason someone seeks out a counselor ultimately rests in their inability to handle the information of their circumstances. After years of working with people I have come to understand that most simply desire the hurting to stop. In fact, the majority of people don't really want to change; they simply want out of the hurt. But a Christian who expects you to provide answers only to his liking is like a foolish person who dives into a polluted lake without knowing what is under the water.

I have also found over the past that what we see on the surface are merely the symptoms of our problems and not the root cause. Much like the iceberg, it is the unseen mass below the surface that represents the real danger.

I have found the process I am about to describe to be effective over the long term in exposing the root of the problem. There is nothing magical in it; mystical perhaps, in that we may not understand how the Holy Spirit performs his surgery in our mind.

"God's ways are not ours"

The prophet Isaiah makes a plea for the troubled soul to "Seek the Lord while He may be found." If we accept that Romans 8:28 is accurate (all things work together for our good), then we must also accept that the difficulties that bring us to seek help have divine origins. Difficult circumstances become the catalyst that moves us to seek God and our destiny of being conformed to the image of His son.

Look at the following words from Isaiah 65:6-11. *"Seek the Lord while He may be found, call upon Him while He is near. Let the wicked forsake his way, and the unrighteous man his thoughts; let him return to the Lord, and He will have mercy on him; and to our God for He will abundantly pardon. For My thoughts are not your thoughts, nor are your ways My ways says the Lord. For as the heavens are higher that the earth, so are My ways higher than your ways, and My thoughts than your thoughts. For as the rain comes down, and the snow from heaven, and do not return there, but water the earth, and make it bring forth and bud, that it may give seed to the sower and bread to the eater, so shall My Word be that goes forth from My mouth; it shall not return to Me void, but it shall accomplish what I please, and it shall prosper in the thing for which I sent it.*

When I reference God's mystical work I am talking about His prerogative as the sovereign creator who acts in accordance with His plan for our lives through events beyond our comprehension. I contend that our difficulties in this life stem mainly from our tendency to take our lives in a direction that is contrary to His plan and purpose.

"His ways are not our ways"

I want to be sure you understand the distinction I make between 'magical and mystical'. The word magical, for some, implies a little hocus pocus, sleight of hand, or simply an illusion. Mystical on the other hand refers to that which is mysterious or unknown. It also implies that there is a way to discover that which is not known. It is the latter that Isaiah is making reference to in this passage. God's work in our life is 'higher' in purpose and destiny. We operate in the physical and temporary; God operates in the spiritual and eternal so that's where his work in us is concentrated.

"There is a season's delayed effect,"

Isaiah gives us an illustration to help us understand how these higher and different ways are to be understood. This passage has often been used to justify strange and difficult circumstances. We are often told to accept circumstances because after all His ways and thoughts are different than ours. We are therefore encouraged to just accept things as they are and trudge forward. I shall propose a different viewpoint using Isaiah's illustration.

First let's examine the image Isaiah presents. The first element is rain and snow. The second is the growth of grain

as a result of the first. The third is the productivity
future plantings and bread for present consumptior
implication is that there is correlation of all the elemen[illegible]
the first there cannot be the other two. As the farmer harvests his crop he sets aside seed for the next season and then turns the bulk over to the baker who produces the bread that both eat for sustenance. They don't complain about the rain and snow because they know without them they would die of starvation. They know that the rain will have a season's delayed effect.

Isaiah records the Lord's comment: "So shall my word be that goes forth from my mouth; it shall not return to me void, but it shall accomplish that which I please, and it shall prosper in the thing whereto I sent it."

As we begin this process of cleansing our mind we need to keep this thought in mind: "God will work through my circumstances and sometimes there will be events that are beyond comprehension; at times he may be doing things that will have a season delayed effect."

"The only way to know for sure the will of God is in retrospection."

There are going to be some unanswered questions as you move forward. This however does not mean that we will be in the dark all the time. Wisdom is needed to know when you are facing a circumstance that is to be accepted and when you are facing one that needs to be challenged or even rejected. We will come back to this thought later. For now we need to understand that we will be fishing in dark and uncharted waters in the beginning. Not only that, but we will not always be confident that we are moving in the right direction. The only way we may know for sure that we went in the right direction will be in retrospect. Time will produce its harvest as the seasons pass.

POUR IN CLEAN WATER

"The cleansing water of the mind is the word of God."

We move now to the next step in the process of restoring our mind, the introduction of a cleansing agent. The restoration process of our lake required that we provide a new inlet for fresh, clean water. The purpose is so that the clean water will mix with the polluted water and provide the agent that will begin to displace the pollution. The cleansing water of the mind is the word of God.

Go back and reread the passage from Isaiah 55:6-11. Pay close attention to the last few verses that inform us that God's (specific) word sent to a (specific) situation will not return to him empty or void, but will succeed in the purpose for which he sent it. We are assured that the word of God will have an effect. Also note that I inserted the word "specific". While this word is not used in the text it does reflect the intent of what God is saying to Israel. This means that we simply cannot take a promise or covenant out of its context in the scripture and use it however we like.

This raises another question, "How do we know when we can claim a word from God as intended for us?" Good question. I will deal with this at some length later, but for now the answer is simple—study! Get into the word. Attend a bible study at church or at someone's home. Listen to ministries on the radio and the television. The internet has vast libraries of resources available.

Recently I was at my son's home in central Georgia and while we were looking up some information on the internet he showed me a site where you can read and download sermons. What a resource! It's like having every preacher's library at your disposal. There is no excuse for you not to become involved in a bible study. Let me assure you that if the Spirit abides in you, you will not be long into a study before you will sense his direction.

"We have a direct statement indicating the work of the word in the church."

If the Isaiah passage were the only one that references this subject it would be sufficient, but there is more. Examine Paul's letter to the Ephesians in 5:25-27

"Husbands, love your wives, just as Christ loved the church and gave himself up for her to make her holy, cleansing her by the washing with water through the word, and to present to himself as a radiant church, without stain or wrinkle or any other blemish, but holy and blameless."

You will be hard pressed to find a more definitive statement on this subject. God's intention, aim, purpose, and even desire are found in this statement. The intention of His giving of His son was for our cleansing to prepare us as a fit bride. The "water of the word" is his agent to perform the feat. Therefore the more of the word of God we pour through our mind the more our mind will be cleansed. Also remember that the more specific the word is the more specific the cleansing will be.

"Do not forget that a new flow of water will stir up the settled pollution."

Remember from our illustration the result of introducing a new agent into our polluted lake stirred up the settled debris on the bottom. That resulted in there being an even worse appearance to the texture of our water. In the same manner, as the word of God begins to run through our mind it will stir up much of what has settled down to the recesses of our subconscious. You will actually begin to remember things long forgotten. Our enemy will use this stirring up of the past to accuse us and try to get us to give up, thinking it is a futile process.

RELEASING THE POLLUTED

"Remember that confession means to be in agreement with"

In the lake illustration, we provided an outlet to drain off the excess as we added clean water (to act as a cleansing agent). If we did not provide this outlet, the lake's level would rise to the point that it washed out its banks, spreading the pollution to the surrounding areas.

The outlet for our mind is confession. Listen to 1st John 1:9: *"If we confess our sins, he is faithful and just and will forgive us our sins and purify us from all unrighteousness."*

Let's examine our part in this process then God's part and the subsequent result. Our task is that of confession. The word confession is a compound word in the Greek. It is made up of the word *homo* meaning self or same, and the word *logomen* meaning word or saying. A literal translation of this word is a "saying that is in agreement with". When we are made aware of something we know is not pleasing to God we are to confess it if we are to be cleansed of it. Therefore to agree with God means we say the same thing about our sin that he does.

First we admit it for what it is. When Joseph was confronted with the opportunity to commit adultery with his master's wife he declared that to do so would be a sin against his master and his God. Taking this as an example, when we sin, our confession should begin with a description of what the act is as well as to whom it is against.

Second we choose to give it up. When the woman who was caught in adultery received her forgiveness from Jesus she was told to, "Go! And sin no more". The passage indicates she was to no longer commit this particular sin. Therefore by confessing a particular sin we are giving it up. We choose to commit it no longer.

Finally we must agree with God that it is no longer a part of us. Remember the passage in Hebrews 10:17 where he promises, *"And their sins and iniquities I will remember no more."* It does not state that he will forget them, but rather that he will not remember them. This is an important distinction, because we, like God, do not forget anything unless there is a disease or injury to our brain. God is not able to forget anything unless he becomes less than omniscient. This is one characteristic of his being.

One quality that a "god" must have is that of knowing all things past, present, and future. We must conclude then that He knew I would sin even before I was born and yet He sent His son to die for me and He chose to save me even knowing how often I would fail.

People will often share with me that part of the reason they don't serve God is because they have "let Him down". I shock them when in reply I ask, "Really? Well how long had you been holding Him up?" After all if our failures let Him down the implication is that we have disappointed Him so now He will have to change His plans. It means we did something He did not know we would do. Think about that. In order for you to disappoint God you have to do something that takes Him by surprise. How can that be possible if He is omniscient?

The truth of the matter is God chose to save you in spite of what He knew you would do, not because of it. And if that is true, then in order for you to be in agreement with God when it comes to confessing your sin, you must choose to not think of yourself in light of your sins. Remember the passage in Romans 8:31-39. Perform a little cleansing right now by turning to this passage and reading it.

I promise you that if you accept this line of thinking the devil will challenge it. He will use religious people more than any others to confuse you. Don't let it happen. What do you have to lose except the guilt and defeat you have been living with?

You will find that as the days pass, the time in between failures will increase and the amount of time that you are resisting the temptation to sin is also increasing. If you persist there will come a time when the amount of success will overshadow the amount of failure.

Remember that it is the Word washing through your mind that is pushing out the filthiness of your past and that, through confession, cleanses your thinking. This process literally changes the way you think. You will begin to think more like your Father God and less like your former father the devil.

TAKING THE PROCESS BELOW THE SURFACE

As this process progresses you become more conscious of the motivations behind your actions and better able to confront your problems. Examine the illustration below:

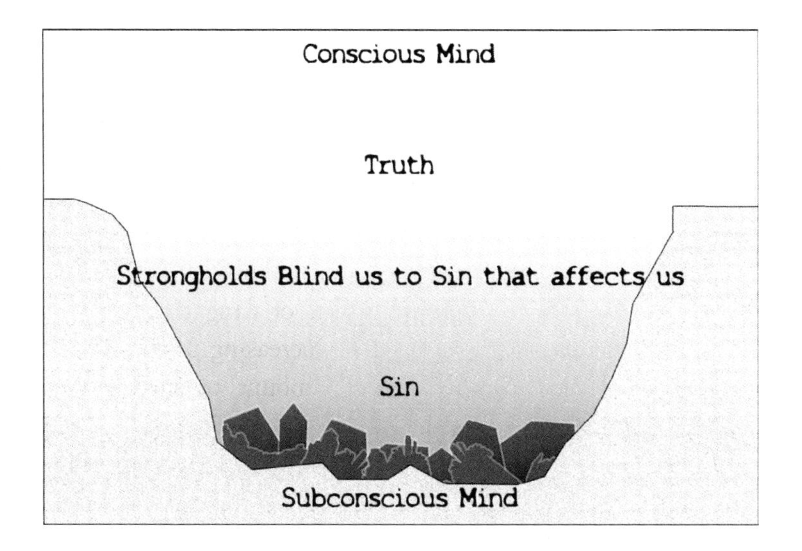

Notice at the top of the image is an area called the conscious mind. It has been said that even the most intelligent people use less than ten percent of their mental capacity. Therefore, the larger portion of the image is committed to the subconscious mind. It is here that all the information we have ever taken in through any of our five senses is stored. In reference to our lake, our consciousness mind would be represented by the section of the water that is clear—that which we can see through. The sub-consciousness mind is represented by the cloudy or polluted portion of water where we are unable to see anything. What enters our mind, either with our awareness or without, soon settles down into our subconscious where we are oblivious to its presence. It's not that we forget this information, but rather that it settles down out of sight and therefore out of our awareness. This is the place where garbage from the past influences our motivations and affect our actions without us realizing that it's happening.

Jesus makes this statement in John 8:32: *"And you shall know the truth, and the truth shall make you free."* Have you ever wondered why you continue to commit some sins without plan or preparation? Allow me to make perhaps a new and startling proposition to you. The reason you continue to practice a particular sin even though you may not want to is because you haven't allowed the truth to sink to the same level in your mind that the sin has. How often are you plagued by a sin in private that you have power over when you are in a public place? Do you use language on the job that you would never consider using in your Sunday school class?

I will never forget the look on my new bride's face when I lost my cool one evening at home and let out a string of obscenities. We had been together for several years and I knew that she would not be accepting of such language, so I refrained from using it around her. As I became more comfortable around her, I lowered my guard until in a fit of anger what was inside flowed out of my mouth. To her credit her reaction made me raise my guard back up. She was quick to let me know that I would not use such language around her. She also told me I should be ashamed of it. I was and it was this encounter that led me to work on cleansing my mind of it.

Look at the following illustration:

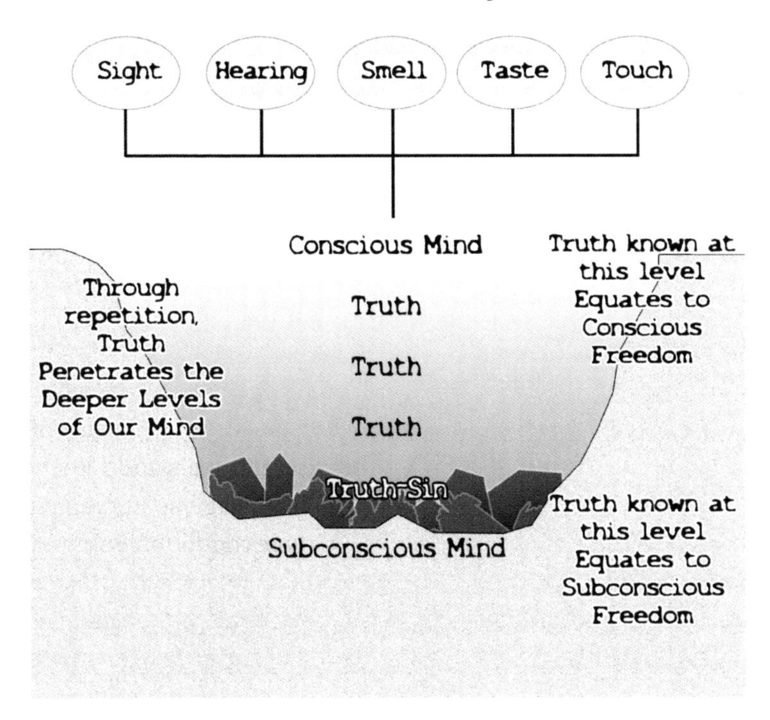

THE TRUTH MUST SETTLE TO THE LEVEL OF BONDAGE

We are literally enslaved by the sins of our past. The degree to which we are in bondage is in direct proportion to the degree of its entry through our conscious mind into our subconscious one. It only stands to reason that we must drive the truth into our subconscious thinking by filtering it again and again through the conscious mind.

This is the reason I stated that when you fail you have to get up and try again—and keep on trying until you are free all the way down to your subconscious. Notice in our oval that every time you consciously do something it goes deeper and deeper into the mind until you do it without thinking. When the truth reaches the same level in the subconscious as the bondage, you will be free. This happened for me again and again. For example when I quit smoking I quit for two minutes and have never smoked since.

Here's how it happened. I came home from work one evening to find that I was now living with an expectant mother. After we had finished our evening meal, Cathy came into the living room and took a snapshot of me with our new instamatic camera as I sat in my easy chair. After it had developed she handed it to me and proudly announced that this was a photograph of the daddy of her baby. I took it, looked at it for a moment, then laid it on the table next to my chair.

A few minutes later I looked over at my image and my eyes rested on the cigarette that was wedged between two fingers. That's all I could see for a few moments. Then a question hit me, "Why do I smoke?" I thought for a moment and realized, "I smoke because I saw my daddy smoke." That raised another question, "Will this baby smoke because it sees me smoke? And what else will this child struggle with because of watching me?" I made up my mind that no matter what it took I would never hear my child say they did something bad or wrong because they saw me doing it.

The next day I announced to everyone on the job that I was going to quit smoking. I received laughs and verbal jabs in response. I was working on a job with my dad and two brothers a few days later. All of us smoked and since I had announced that I was quitting all I had heard from them was ridicule.

That next day I bought a five pack of cigars and when I got the urge I would light one up, take a few puffs, and put it out. About mid morning I was in the back of the house we were working on with no one around me. So I lit up my cigar, took a few puffs, put it out and looked at it in disgust. I sat down on my work bench and shook my head and began to cry within. I anguished with the thought that a leaf could control my life and began to pray and ask God why I could not quit.

I sat there, looked at my watch and realized that I had been still for two minutes when a thought occurred to me, "How long has it been since you last smoked?"

"Two minutes."

"Well, if you can go two minutes, surely you can go four." So I sat there and watched until four minutes clicked by. I thought, "If I can go four, I can surely go eight." Again I sat and watched eight minutes click by. If I can go eight I can make it to sixteen. So I marked the time on my watch when the sixteen would expire, forgot about my desire to smoke and went back to work.

I know this sounds overly simplified, but it is quite literally the way I quit. I kept doubling the minutes until they became hours, the hours days, then weeks and months. By the time six months had passed I no longer kept track nor needed too. You see, by the time six months had passed, the thought that I could make it for a certain time frame without smoking had reached the same level in my subconscious as the desire to smoke, so I was free.

I had tried to quit smoking many times before, but always started again. It wasn't until I agreed with God as to why I smoked and the need to not let it pass through to another generation that I found the motivation needed to make it real. Sometimes we have to confess something for quite a while before we realize why we are doing it.

This brings us to the last part of our illustration, the removal of the garbage buried in the depths of our mind...

hidden at the bottom of the lake. Some of us have buried things in our past and forgotten about them, but they are still there and they can be formidable obstacles that will have to be dealt with. Only those who are truly committed to this process will go on from here. The removal of things in our past sometimes means the removal of a part of the person we have become—and that can be scary.

We are moving into what Paul in his letter to the Corinthians calls "strongholds".

"A stronghold is a mental image that is false but is believed to be true."

Have you ever committed a sin you did not want to commit and tell yourself you will not commit even while you are committing it? Does that sound confusing? If it does then you have never come to grips with a stronghold in your mind. That doesn't necessarily mean you don't have one. It simply means you have never been aware of it.

We all have false images we believe to be true and it isn't until we begin to cleanse our mind and give control of our thought processes over to the Spirit that they become apparent. Let's look at the passage where we find this word stronghold, Second Corinthians 10:4-6.

"For the weapons of our warfare are not carnal but mighty in God for pulling down strongholds, casting down imaginations and every high thing that exalts itself against the knowledge of God, and bringing every thought captive to the obedience of Christ, and having a readiness to punish all disobedience when our obedience is fulfilled.

We see several things in this passage. First is the nature of our struggle—it is not in the flesh but in the mind. Paul tells us that our weapon is not carnal or in the flesh, but rather in God's power to destroy strongholds. These imaginations (mental images) that are contrary to the knowledge of God must be toppled and then all other thoughts brought under his control. Once this is accomplished the flesh is corrected.

The imagery Paul uses here is that of taking a besieged city. In his day the Romans would surround a walled city and cut off its supply lines. As the city weakened because of a lack of supplies the attacks would begin. Before the walls could be scaled, however, the towers along its perimeter, from which archers would shoot their arrows and boiling oil be poured onto the warriors below, had to be taken. These towers had to be torn down or, at the minimum, rendered useless. Once this was done the walls were compromised and the gates would be opened.

Most conquering armies up until the time of the Romans would take a city and destroy it. The Romans however would take a city and stop the death and destruction as soon as possible. They would leave the city with its civic and economic structure intact, but leave a remnant of soldiers behind. These soldiers were left to keep the now defeated city in line. This ingenious strategy allowed the Romans to have a continual flow of bounty instead of merely a one-time ransacking of goods. This was the Roman road to world domination.

Paul draws a parallel to the Roman conquerors and teaches us that God tears down false images in our mind of who we are, who he is, and how things are to be. Then he establishes control over our thoughts so they fall in line with how things should be. As the word of God flows through our mind and establishes a foothold in our subconscious, we begin to act more the way God designed us. When we hit a dead end it is because we have come up against a stronghold.

The removal of a stronghold does not come easily. First it must be exposed. That is what happened to me when I came to the realization that I smoked because I had watched my father smoke. It was the early seventies and I was twenty years old. I had smoked as long as I could remember. I remember being caught by my parents when I was five. That's quite shocking until you realize that every little boy emulates his father. I was no exception.

The situation explained earlier was the end of a long struggle against what I knew was a nasty and health damaging habit. I became a Christian shortly before my eighteenth birthday and even before then I despised the habit. Yet I could not shake it. I had spent countless hours praying and asking the Lord to help me rid myself of it, all to no effect.

I remember as a Sunday school teacher of youth in our church dealing with the subject of being the temple of the Holy Spirit. After class I was standing outside the educational building at the smoking pit when one of my students came walking up. She looked at me and my cigarette and said, "You know what Brother Charles, the Holy Spirit is inside you doing this..." She proceeded to pinch her nose shut with one hand and with the other she fanned the imaginary smoke in front of her.

Instances such as this and numerous others humiliated me and yet I could not kick the habit. However when I came to the truth of why I smoked I was able to stop. Until that day on that job I could not see myself without a cigarette. What the Spirit did that day was give me an image of myself without a cigarette in my hand.

In summary:

- Take the necessary steps to stop the pollution of your thought process.
- Begin to run the water of the word through your mind with prayer.

- As you become aware of sin confess it in the prescribed manner.
- Confront the strongholds, tear them down, and become obedient.

Remember that the enemy will let us witness, go to church, read Christian books, and a myriad of other Christian activities, but when we set out to study the word and pray he unleashes the hounds of hell to distract us. Knowing this, we should make the word and prayer a priority. The more difficult it is for you to concentrate and pray, the more likelihood there is that you have strongholds you need to overcome.

SECTION TWO
THE TIMELINE OF PHYSIOLOGICAL AND PSYCHOLOGICAL DEVELOPMENT

In section one I mentioned how sharing the process of my son's healing drew Gayle to me for help and how the teaching tool I call Lake Mind came into existence because of her need to understand the importance of allowing the Word to flow through her mind and have its affect.

In this chapter I will share another tool I call the Timeline of Development that grew out of two struggles. The first struggle was personal and very subjective on two fronts. The second was more objective and universal.

The struggle I related to in the introduction was my difficulty with the process of sanctification. I was not given the tools to handle the transformation I needed nor was I given a concept as to the struggle and time it was going to take to change.

Actually, all the testimonies I was hearing had the "instant healing" sound to them. We would have testimony time every few Sunday nights and some brother would stand up and mention a sin that I was struggling with and declare, "Yep. Thirty years ago I did this and then the Lord saved me and I don't do it no more." I would sit there and wonder why God granted him such immediate relief and was making me struggle. If I was foolish enough to confide in someone about this discrepancy the response was to chide me for attacking the integrity of the one testifying or tell me if I was continuing to be plagued with this sin I was not serious about changing or not saved to begin with.

I knew I was sincere and that I was God's child, therefore the first personal front was "Why am I not able to immediately overcome certain difficulties and others seem to have no problem?" That lead me to question our "One size fits all" method of evangelism and discipleship (which doesn't "fit all" after all).

The universal struggle is related to that fallacy:

"Is there a universal way of teaching about the struggles a new believer will face that brings enlightenment and help without becoming just another 'one size fits all' system?"

While involved in developing a methodology through the timeline, the second front on the personal/subjective arose. My son was diagnosed with epilepsy and a new wrinkle was added, "How does our growth—or lack thereof—affect the sanctification process of those we are involved with?"

If you are a 'thinking' person as opposed to a 'doing' person, you are now questioning my ability—if not my sanity—in attempting to pull this off. However, I ask you to give me the benefit of the doubt and read on. If you are a "doer", please hold back on practicing what you read until you have completed the reading of this book.

"Why the Struggle Varies For Every Believer Even Though We Share a Common Salvation"

If you failed to read the introduction you will need to go back and read it as I pick my story back up at this juncture. Walking away from Christianity was not an option when I was 19 and it will never be an option for any believer. Paul wrote to the believers in Philippi, "*I thank my God upon every remembrance of you, always in every prayer of mine making request for you all with joy, for your fellowship in the gospel from the first day until now, being confident of this very thing, that He who has begun a good work in you will complete it until the day of Jesus Christ."*

Read that again!

Now read again beginning about halfway at the word 'being'! Do you realize what Paul is saying? Allow me to paraphrase that last half. "If I'm sure of anything, I'm sure of this: if God started something in you, He will finish the task!" If you were struggling with your walk with God and were standing in front of me, I would grab both your shoulders, look you in the eye and, based on these verses, say "You are going to make it!"

If you can know that and hold onto it you can endure anything.

The back door to our churches is as wide open as the front door because of our lack of engagement in the struggle new believers face when they join our assemblies. Those who 'stick' with us and join the flow of our system of worship and service are already living with a level of self-discipline that allows them to join the stream of activities in the church where acceptance is found. If those who come into the front door of the church do not find acceptance, or if they just don't fit in for some reason, it won't be long before they will discover the back door. This is not what I want to write about, but it cannot be avoided if there is ever going to be a marked change in our fulfilling of the commission Jesus gave us just before He went to prepare His Father's house so could join Him.

Had someone from my church taken me by the shoulders and told me with intensity and sincerity I was going to make it 'no matter what' and made me believe it, I would have not experienced those three months of futility I describe in the introduction.

When I came back to the church and fell back into the flow of things the church was not any different—but I was.

Holding on to the fact that if I sought the Lord He would reward the effort, coupled with knowing that He would work 'all' things for my good, I came upon these verses in Philippians and gained the assurance that I was going to make it. All I needed to do was hold on, to persevere.

Self-discipline, or the lack thereof, is the key to the variation in struggle that people experience when they enter the faith. Even with the struggles I had because of my past sinfulness I came back and made it, not because of my own effort, but because when God starts something, He finishes it. That's what the scripture teaches. So then the question is "Why don't we teach it?" Could it be because too many congregations are dependent on the pastor and staff to lead them in worship, bible study, and outreach?

At the time of this writing, I attend a large church with a very aggressive and evangelistic program. We are on television and radio and have numerous ministries to the community. When you join our church, you are counseled and prayed with, then given information about the various groups in the church available to help you become a part of things. We have recovery groups for everything from singles, to couples, to parenting, to financial counseling, divorce, being widowed, abortion, unwed pregnancy, and probably some I don't know about. Our pastor is educated, dedicated, conservative, and effective in drawing people to the cross. And I could go on and on. We are indeed a working congregation. But our back door stands wide open.

Evangelism isn't about masses—it's about individuals. It isn't about the invitation time. It's about what got the individual to the place of commitment and how they move on from there. As long as our focus in evangelism is on the invitation and church program involvement we will continue to have an open back door. To rectify this, our focus must shift so that it is on the full spectrum of what the spiritual life is. Evangelism isn't just Roman's road unless you include all the doctrines found in Paul's letter.

For the most part, the programs in the church have separated evangelism and discipleship, when in fact evangelism—telling the gospel—is one of the facets of discipleship. Evangelism is not the program for building the church; discipleship is.

Examine with me how the Holy Spirit gave the program of building the church through the eyes of Matthew.

"And Jesus came and spoke to them saying, "All authority has been given to Me in heaven and on earth. Go therefore and make disciples of all nations, baptizing them in the name of the Father and of the Son, and of the Holy Spirit, teaching them to observe all things that I have commanded you; and lo, I am with you always, even to the end of the age."

I have checked numerous Greek sources and all agree the subject of this commission, 'you', is implied in 'go therefore'. The predicate is also the only verb in this command, 'make disciples'. Baptizing and teaching them are modifiers. This even comes through when you break down the 'Great Commission' in its English translation. In other words, the focus of Jesus' last words was for us to be duplicating ourselves. That is what being a disciple is. Therefore evangelism is not fulfillment of the great commission unless it includes bringing along a novice in the practice of the Christian faith to the point that he too reaches out and brings someone along. When I tried to go out the back door of my church, no one even knew there was anything wrong simply because I was no one's disciple. I was an excellent church member and that's all anyone knew or cared about. Sanctification thrives within discipleship and struggles in its absence.

If you feel that I am being unfair, or that your church is the exception to the rule, I challenge you to pull out the church roll from a year or so ago and check the attendance. If you are a church leader and this offends you, you probably need to be offended. James commands us to "Be not many teachers knowing that we shall receive the greater condemnation". If you know anything about hermeneutics then you know the accuracy of these statements.

If you are still with me, I promise to get down off my soapbox and get back on track with our subject. Just allow me this: The adjustment that most churches need to make in order for discipleship to become the modus operandi rather than an option is merely a change of emphasis. When making disciples is the church's primary emphasis, the first order of business becomes telling the good news to enough individuals until we find a person who wants to follow Jesus. Then their training begins, which includes teaching them to share their faith and make disciples.

Compare that to the emphasis of getting people 'saved'. When getting a person to the place of commitment is our purpose, and they make a public commitment, our objective has been accomplished. Therefore we move on to the next lost soul who needs to 'get saved'. Call me a simpleton if you like, but I believe the former accomplishes more than the latter ever will. Ok...enough about that.

In this chapter our objective is to understand the stages of human development and how the cross and the process of regeneration affect us during these stages. We will also make application of the process we saw in the previous chapter and show how we are affected.

Before we begin, though, I need to share an event in my life that God used to drive me to a period of study and prayer that resulted with the development of this book. This event will take some time to share, but I believe relating it will encourage and motivate you.

"His eyes began to twitch and roll back as he went into an epileptic seizure."

My son was three and a half years old and I was the pastor of a small group of believers trying to start a new church on the north side of our city. Truthfully, I joined this group of believers without praying and seeking the will of God in the matter. Two weeks after I began meeting with them I knew it was a mistake, yet I stayed for almost a year because I didn't want to disappoint or discourage the work. Not leaving, however, became a bigger mistake.

Several months later our son began to have mental time-outs. A glazed look would come over his eyes and he would stare up toward the sky or ceiling. Next the muscles around his eyes began twitching and his eye would roll up. We took him to his pediatrician, who immediately sent us to see an epilepsy specialist. The mere mention of epilepsy sent chills up my spine.

After several months had passed, we had seen three different doctors and tried several different types of medicine. Still the seizures persisted with the medicine having little or no effect except to make our son a zombie. I was worried, my wife cried a lot and family and friends began to counsel how this was our "cross"—we needed to accept it and learn to live with it.

This counsel, received from the family of God, shocked me. Defeat was the order of the day and it seemed as if I was on an island when I talked of expecting God to heal my son. I refused to accept this disease as having been sanctioned by

God and set myself to prayer and a study of the word of God with full expectation of an answer.

My prayer partner and best friend was with me one morning and he posed this question, "Charles, I know you don't want to accept that Chuck having this disease is a part of God's plan, but what if it is?" I looked at him and declared to him that I was going to bang on heavens door so long and so hard that the Lord was either going to heal Chuck or tell me to shut up and accept it. I then said, "If that happens he will give me the grace to accept it. But I want you to know Chuck having to live with this is the last thing I will accept, so until he tells me it's His plan I am going to pray for his healing."

So I prayed. I fasted and prayed. I read and studied everything I could about healing. I also studied epilepsy. I would go into my study in the morning and put on a stack of praise records, put on my headphones and pray the word of God. Early in this pattern of praying I was drawn to Mark chapter nine where there is the account of a father approaching Jesus about healing his son.

Then one of the crowd answered and said, "Teacher, I brought you my son who has a mute spirit. And whenever it seizes him, it throws him down; he foams at the mouth, gnashes his teeth, and becomes rigid. So I spoke to your disciples, that they should cast it out, but they could not." He answered him and said, "O faithless generation, how long shall I be with you?" Bring him to me." Then they brought him to Him. And when he saw Him, immediately the spirit convulsed him, and he fell on the ground and wallowed, foaming at the mouth. So he asked the father, "How long has this been happening to him?" And he said, "From childhood. And often he has thrown him both into the fire and into the water to destroy him. But if you can do anything, have compassion on us and help us." Jesus said unto him, "If you can believe, all things are possible to him who believes." Immediately the father cried out to him, "Lord I believe, help my unbelief!" When Jesus saw that the people came running together, He rebuked the unclean spirit, saying to it, "Deaf and dumb spirit, I command you, come out of him and enter him no more!" Then the spirit cried out, convulsed him greatly, and came out of him. And he became as one dead, so that many said, "He is dead." But Jesus took him by the hand and lifted him up, and he arose. And when he had come into the house, His disciples asked Him privately, "Why could we not cast it out?" So He said to them, "This kind can come out by nothing but prayer and fasting."

Now this is not a discourse on healing or demon possession, but rather to show you how my attitude about God healing my son was reinforced by several things in this passage.

First, look at the persistence of the father. He had already been to the disciples without results, so he comes to Jesus and the response he receives is a rebuke. After the situation is explained, he is simply told to believe and believing will bring healing. To that he responds, "Lord I believe; help my unbelief!"

To me he was saying, "I have already expended all the faith I have and yet there is at the same time this unbelief abiding with me. You dispel unbelief and my belief will take over." So I began to pray that the Lord would deal with any unbelief that I might have. Then I increased my periods of fasting. Normally I would fast Mondays, so I increased my fast from Monday morning until Wednesday evening. This continued for almost a year. Along the way, using the principle of Lake Mind, I began to see things about myself that brought a lot of confession and repentance.

Shortly before my son began to have his seizures I had begun to seriously attack my thought life in the area of lust. I struggled greatly with images in my mind from my past involvement with pornography and had gone for counseling about my problem. The man I saw at that time introduced me to the possibility of ancestral sin with its visitation on the children as is seen in the Ten Commandments (Exodus 20). I must admit that I was highly skeptical at first. Yet, after one visit with him and a time of prayer and confession of the sins of my ancestors, I found freedom. I not only gained control over my thoughts but other associated things as well.

Then, about the time I felt I was getting close to an answer with Chuck's situation, I came under a mental attack that was stronger than ever before. It seemed the harder I prayed the more I was attacked in my thoughts with all sorts of lust and perversion. Once again I sought counsel. This time it was another brother who after a time concluded that the trouble I was having with my thoughts was related to the problem Chuck was having. At first I denied any connection. Finally I prayed with him and renounced my past involvement with pornography and was set free from all that I had been wrestling with. I had originally sought this mans counsel because of Chuck and had been disappointed when things went the way they did. This brother shared with me that he sensed that I was close to an answer and he encouraged me to continue. Things were improving, so I kept going, seeking healing for my son.

Several days after this, I was praying when, in my mind's eye, I remembered an event that occurred when I was about seven. I saw myself as a youngster discovering a relative's stash of pornography. I realized that the sin of this relative had opened the door for me and that at an early age I had become hooked on pornography. After this confession, Chuck showed mark improvement.

About three weeks later I was once again praying, when I remembered an accident about a year earlier when Chuck fell out of a chair and landed on his head. We were all concerned but he seemed to be ok. However, it was a few days later that the seizures began. We told the doctors about this but they all dismissed it. A chiropractor friend, though, felt there was a connection and began treatment. Results were limited—but at least there were results. As I recalled the scene and saw him fall, I sensed the Lord convicting me that I was being disobedient by staying with that group, so I repented and confessed my sin of being out of His will at the time of Chuck's fall.

Later that same evening, I watched as Chuck again went into a seizure. I don't know why, but for some reason this time I very quietly told it to stop in the name of Christ. Chuck came out of the seizure and said, "Stop what Daddy?" I could hardly believe it. I called my wife into the room and shared with her what happened. So we began to watch him. We saw no more seizures for several weeks. Then one evening he went into another seizure and immediately I demanded that it stop in the name of Christ and return no more. Chuck has been seizure free for twenty plus years. Hallelujah!

Obviously a lot of what transpired has been omitted for the sake of time and also relevance to our subject. These omissions are also because of the nature of the opposition we faced and the sensitivity of the subject. In a controlled setting I go into much more of the detail concerning the aspect of spiritual warfare as I am able to control the dialogue. To be explicit in writing at this point is not wise, so if the situation you face demands that you know more, you may want to contact me personally. I will be more than happy to help in any way I can.

As you may realize, this kind of prayer and fasting is not the norm in our churches today. When you move into the realm of prayer you are moving into the spiritual realm. The opposition you experience will intensify in direct proportion to the activity you exert. Therefore you must prepare yourself in the defensive posture we briefly examined in Ephesians 6:10-18. The armor listed there has to do with your being, not your doing. The enemy will attack you on these fronts; truthfulness, righteousness, preparedness, knowledge, and the scripture. You can expect the enemy to exploit any weakness you have in order to divert your prayer and fasting.

The attack of the enemy that comes against you will be designed by him to stop you from seeking the assistance of God in your dilemma. God, however, will use these attacks to lead you in changing those areas of your life that do not measure up to the standard He has set for you. Don't be deterred by this, but rather allow the Spirit to change you.

Understand this...if the devil cannot defeat you, he may try to defeat someone close whose defeat will defeat you. I recommend that you pray for the protection of those around you as vigorously as you pray for yourself.

The distress we experienced because of my son's disease led to a year long battle against the lust that had controlled my thought life for as long as I could remember. When I discovered the subconscious stronghold that the enemy was using against me (my relative's involvement with pornography) and confessed his sin and its influence in the development of my sexual identity, I was transformed. I grew up with a perverted understanding of what sexual relations were intended to be. That warped image of sexuality almost destroyed my marriage. It wasn't that I didn't know what was right; I simply couldn't make my mind conform. Subsequently, after the confession of my relative's sin, the old patterns became perverse, the right knowledge fell into place, and my actions followed.

To sum it up, God allowed the attack on my son (because of my sin in not following his leadership to leave this group) as incentive to draw me into a time of prayer and fasting where I discovered the root cause for my struggle with lust. Once the stronghold was confessed and dealt with, I saw the disease in my son disappear. A direct result of the study I did during this time is the information you are receiving in this book.

THE TIMELINE

The timeline of spiritual, psychological, and physiological development came to me as a culmination a various sources. I don't know of any one author or resource that I can give credit to nor do I know if what follows is a duplication of someone else's work. I do know that it is an accurate understanding of our development and is sufficient to assist us in this study.

GENERAL NOTES

Each section we are going to examine will have three main distinctions:

1. Dependency—We are seeking to establish both personal responsibility and the responsibility of those in charge of our care;
2. Mental Image—We see images in our brain, not words. We act and react with our world from three basic images: our image of God, our image of others, and our self-image;
3. Chief character trait—Which character trait is established in each stage along with its interaction with the other stages.

Birth and Infancy to Early Childhood

Birth	3-5	10-12	18-23
85% of Personality Total Dependency Image of God			

The time of our birth up until 3-5 years of age is the formative years of our personality. It is during this time of total dependency that up to 85% of our personality is formed. Also during this time, because of our dependency on others coupled with our lack of cognitive memory, we develop our image of God. In addition, we must not rule out genetics and ancestry.

We know that we get our physical attributes from our parents and, because of our ability to map DNA, we are even able to trace specific traits back countless generations. Studies made with children who have never known their genetic parents have shown that personality traits can be passed down. One such study I observed brought male triplets together after they were grown. None of the three knew of the others and were raised in different parts of the United States and yet when they met for the first time in their early twenties, their personalities were almost identical. It was noted by those conducting this study that had they been raised together they all three would have developed different and distinct personalities.

Besides physical and psychological influences on the development of personality, there are spiritual ones. The bible teaches us that we are born with the nature of our father, Adam. In Romans 5, Paul tells us that when Adam rebelled we were in him and thus fell with him. Back in the eighties, with the discovery DNA, it was noted that there were certain characteristics that are identical in all humans. I remember seeing a news report where this information was being released in a news conference. When asked to explain what this meant, the scientist stated that it meant all humans came from the same father. Several years later another universal characteristic was discovered and the answer came back that we all came from one woman. It's amazing that thousands of years after Eden, science comes to a conclusion stated as fact in the first book of the bible.

Birth	3-5	Childhood 10-12	18-23
	85% of Personality Total Dependency Image of God	Values learned by actions and instructions of role models Conscience is developed Interdependency	

Our next stage begins as communication skills are developed. Note that we draw a line that covers several years, because it takes several years to begin to effectively communicate with our children. Please understand these lines are drawn for the sake of study and are not hard lines where one particular aspect of development stops and another begins. Just as our communications skills may continue for a good deal of the remainder of our lives, so will certain aspects of our personality be developed for years after we have left the first stage.

The principle trait developed during the childhood years is our value system with the result of a conscience. Some call this an inner voice or guide. Our values are the basis of our ethics and morals. An individual's ethics are the foundation or support structure of their moral actions. Morals may change based upon the situation or circumstances we find ourselves facing each day. Our ethics however stay the same.

For example, Corrie Ten Boom was a Christian that lived in Germany during the time of Hitler. She ended up in a concentration camp because of the assistance she gave to the Jews Hitler was persecuting. Being a Christian, her ethic concerning being honest and telling the truth came under attack when agents of the government questioned her about her Jewish neighbors. She lied to these agents about the whereabouts of her friends in order to save their lives. Even though it was contrary to the ethic of truthfulness, she could not morally betray her friends. The ethic of the value of life itself caused her to act in a way contrary to the pure ethic of telling the truth.

We are taught our values by actions and instructions of our role models. We learn these values predominately through observation. Instructions are given normally in the earlier years of this stage in the way of correction.

Take the situation of two young children playing together with their own toys. One child may forcefully take the toys away from his playmate, causing him to cry or even retaliate. The caretaker will step in and correct the injustice and instruct the offender concerning the error of his ways. This puts information into the child's mind along with the actions and helps this child put value to both. So, as the child grows and learns, this information settles into the recesses of his subconscious mind and there begins to formulate a conscience which will guide future activity.

The word 'conscience' is a compound word made from *con,* meaning all or together and *science*, meaning knowledge. Our use of the word indicates that what some call an inner voice is a message that has combined all the information in our mind and synthesized it into a simple instruction. All of this takes place in the subconscious part of our mind.

Therefore when Corrie Ten Boom lied to Hitler's henchmen, she was doing the right thing. She understood without hesitation that these fellows did not deserve the truth because of how they would act upon it.

Sounds confusing, doesn't it? Life is complicated at best. Add to this the fact that our culture demands neutrality on the subject of values and it creates a society that is not only confused, but also morally bankrupt. That is why it's important that we teach these things to our children and set an agenda that is aggressive in influencing those in our culture as well.

I often find myself in controversial situations in public when I speak out against that which I find immoral. Part of this kind of reaction has to do with my being an extravert. I like to think, however, that it is the kind of response we all should be having as part of following Jesus' command for us to be light and salt to a dying world. (Sorry about the soapbox speech. I can't help it. I'm a preacher. It's a compulsion that comes with the calling.)

The interactions that take place during this stage between a child and those who have the influence over him cause the development of the image of others. Our image of others falls into categories of being parental, fraternal and societal. The main characteristic of the parental image has to do with authority and the exertion of it or the need for submission to it. This image finds transference in our culture as we move from the home to the church, school, and then the work place. If our parents are inconsistent and allow us to get away with things at home, we will attempt the same at school and then at work.

The frame of mind set forth during this stage is one of interdependency. Beginning with potty training early in this stage to the point of being able to have an allowance and make other decisions that affect their life, the child is not yet independent, but neither is he dependent for much of what he experiences.

Birth	3-5	10-12 Puberty to Young Adult	18-23
85% of Personality Total Dependency Image of God	Values learned by actions and instructions of role models Conscience is developed Interdependency	Values experimentation Independence Adopt adult role Self-image	

As my own children reached the end of the childhood stage and were entering the next, I sat each one down and gave them the "You are about to become an adult!" speech. I will never forget the look on my daughter's face as I began to give her this speech. I was surprised one evening when at eleven years old she made a request and wanted a response. I don't remember the exact nature of her request, but I will forever remember her at that moment.

I was engrossed in a television program when she made her request while standing in the doorway to her bedroom, which was behind the couch I was laying on. I looked over my shoulder and told her to go to bed, saying something about getting back to her later. I sat there for a few minutes when I felt her eyes boring a hole in the back of my head. I turned and looked at her for a second, then she forcefully said, "Well, what's it going to be!"

I sat up, pointed my finger at her and informed her that I had spoken and her only response, if she knew what was good for her, was to go to bed.

I sat there for a few more minutes, steaming at the fact that she was so bold. It dawned on me that something new was happening and my answer to her had been inadequate, which was confirmed a short time later when my wife informed me that Joy was becoming a woman. So I began to pray and prepare for the speech. My wife got the privilege of delivering the sex education and I was privileged to deliver the adulthood part.

Several days after the sex talk (after she quit looking at me with unbelief) she and I sat down and had our discussion. I began by talking about pre-marital sex, alcohol, drugs, and tobacco, and their easy availability and ended with, "Joy you can do as much of these things as you desire." And let it sink in. When she realized that I had just given her permission to be involved with those things, she got a shocked look on her face and exclaimed, "What do you mean, daddy?"

I was quiet for a few more seconds while looking down at the floor. Then I looked up at her and said, "You have my permission to do as many of those things as you have seen your mother and I do." She smiled as she understood what I was telling her. I went on to explain to her that even though she had not witnessed those things in our lives, she could still do them and perhaps hide them from us, but she could not hide from God nor could she hide from the consequences that would come with them.

From there I began to inform her just how her mother and I were going release her into adulthood. I used the illustration of a rope being tied around her waist with us holding the coil of it in our hands. I laid out school activities, dating, make-up, driving and most of the adult activities she would begin to experience. I related to her that as we let out rope she was invited to take up the slack. She was then told that the rope would continue to be released only as she showed herself to be acting responsible in each new endeavor. I then assured her that deviation and rebellion would be met first with a stopping of the release of the rope and if she continued in that vein we would take rope back. I very humbly, gladly and with parental pride can share with you that both my son and daughter navigated this next stage safely.

The "R" word—REBELLION

The greatest fear we have as parents is that our child will rebel in their teens and destroy their lives. In a lot of cases such a fear comes from their own experience as a teen. This time of life is difficult at best. Parents will tell their teenagers to act like adults one moment and treat them like children in the next. Likewise, a teen will demand to be treated as an adult while throwing a temper tantrum like a three year old. As a parent, you enter these years with fear only if you haven't done a good job preparing for this time.

I can tell you now every area your child will rebel in. A bold statement you say. Well here it is: Your child will rebel in every area in which what you said to them was contradicted by what they saw you do. You taught them your values by word and deed and the saying goes, "What you do speaks louder than what you say." You know this is true. All you need do is reflect on your own past and that of your parents.

In my own life this was certainly true. The greatest incentive I had as a young Christian was that I did not want my children to struggle to overcome the vices and habits that plagued me as a teen. I remember well my dad lecturing me on the bad consequences of smoking, all the while he had one stuck between his fingers. I know he meant well and his intentions were as sincere as mine have been with my own children. Yet I didn't believe him at the time. What he did spoke louder than what he said and you and I are no different.

Don't be discouraged. It is not too late to begin again with your child. Even if they are already into their teen years, there is hope. Your actions still speak louder than words, but only if you become consistent from this time forward. I must admit that you may have to wait a while longer for results, but it will be worth the effort and the wait. After all, you can have a fresh start with that wonderful gift from God, grandchildren.

"Me do it!"

Speaking of grandchildren, as I write this Joy's husband, Nathan, privileged us with a grandson when he married our daughter. Since then the two of them worked together to give us Natalie. Natalie is two years old and beginning to talk up a storm. One of her favorite things to say when you try to help her do almost anything is, "Me do it!" and yes, it is usually spoken with an exclamation point.

This attitude of independence begins when they are very young and continues throughout life. We are, after all, designed by God to be creative and resourceful and that is the source of this mindset. Unfortunately though, because of the fall we experienced with our father Adam, we exercise it illegitimately. From learning to feed themselves instead of being fed (one of Natalie's "me do its") up to "Dad, I can drive myself to school?" our children are legitimately exercising their independence. It's when they overstep the boundaries we parents have established that they have difficulties.

It's like the time when I was fourteen and an air conditioning contractor working on our home asked if I knew how to drive. I quickly assured him that I had been driving for years. With that answer, he handed me a dollar and requested that I drive to the store for a couple of cokes. As I was pulling into the driveway in my dad's truck, my dad came out of the house and confronted me concerning my trip. The contractor admitted that he had made the request without thinking about whether or not I was licensed and he apologized. My father's response was to inform me that I knew I was taking advantage of the situation and I was punished. I knew he was right, but I wanted to do it. I don't know how I thought I would get away with it. I suppose I felt the joy of driving was worth the risk of getting caught.

That's what the struggle with gaining independence is all about—the cost. If we are wise as parents, we will help our children assume the independence of their future adult roles gradually, realizing the cost.

SELF IMAGE

Just as our helplessness formulates our image of God and our interactions with role models develops our image of others, so the establishing of our independence is what forges our self image.

The experimentation of our values played out in the decisions we make in this stage of life gives us vivid memories. Memories that have consequences we have to face up to and live with, both good and bad, often determine how we move forward as adults. We are building a reputation that will go with us throughout life.

Mary the mother of Jesus can attest to this. Even though it has lost its stigma, an unwed mother and the bastard she brings into this world will be remembered long after the pregnancy. If you don't believe me, just ask Jesus. One of the accusations the Pharisees leveled at our Lord was, "We don't know who his father is." It was their way of slandering him and calling him a bastard.

We operate daily out of our self image. If we see ourselves as being capable and competent, that's how we act. Being insecure and unsure of ourselves will cause us to shrink back and shy away from those things we may need to do. If you see yourself as a failure, you will not attempt much because of the fear of failing again. You will stay safely within the areas where you can be assured of success, or at least that your failures will escape discovery.

The reverse is true as well. Confidence goes a long way in motivating us to step out and act.

"Sex is not a four letter word"

That statement is logical, isn't it? You of course know what I am referring to. Sex is not a bad thing. Outside of the parameters of God's intended purpose, however, it can be devastating and in the development of our self-image it can make us or break us.

Our identity is based in our sexuality. After all, God made us male and female. Sex was intended for the sexes. It was designed by the creator to be the bonding agent between a man and his wife. Outside of the context of marriage, however, it can potentially be the most damning of experiences in our development. Within the bounds of God's design, it confirms us, strengthens us, liberates us, fulfills us, and gives us the confidence to take on our world. Bet you have never heard anything like that on Oprah or Donahue.

Our sexual identity is not forged in our experiences during this stage alone, though. Our parents were laying the foundation for it from the very beginning of our existence. The image of God that is being impressed on us in the first stage of our development is one that is both male and female. God exhibits both male and female characteristics. He is portrayed as the masculine provider, protector, and sustainer as well as the feminine comforter, nourisher, and caregiver. I make these statements not to stir up a controversy by tagging God as a man or woman or even as being bisexual. My understanding is that the personality of God is displayed in the Bible as being primarily masculine. Jesus was a man for that matter and the first person of the Godhead is called, "Father". The Genesis account in chapters one and two informs us that we are made in His image. It says that He created man (the Hebrew uses the term Adam for man which is a reference to mankind as a whole), male and female.

As our earthly father takes us up in his arms when we are infants he impresses a masculine image on us with his deep voice and calloused hands. As we grow he's the one who lifts us high in the air with power sometimes throwing us up in the air and catching us. We learn that this being is powerful and sometimes to be feared, yet trusted.

Our mother on the other hand takes us to her breast and nourishes us. She holds us with gentleness, with soft hands, and a tender voice.

In the treatment we receive from this team called 'Adam' we have the image of a God who is powerful, strong, one to be feared and yet we can trust him. At the same time we are learning that he will show us compassion, tenderness, and mercy all the while sustaining us with nourishment.

Examine the chart below.

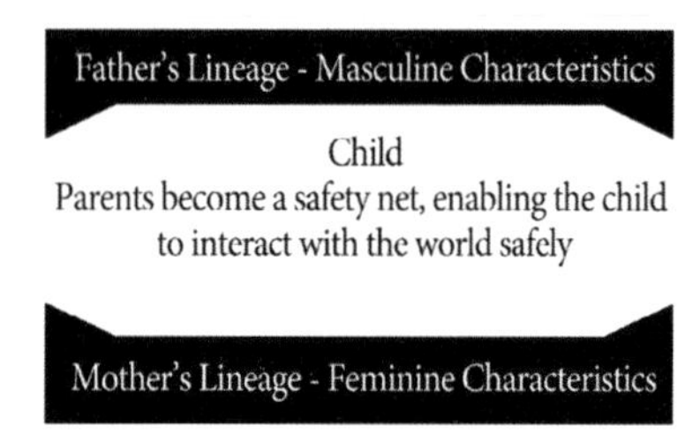

Infancy/Toddlerhood	Childhood	Adolescence
Birth 3-5	10-12	18-23
Conception		
Image of God Total Dependence 85% of Personality	Image of Others Interdependence Values Formed Actions & Instructions of Role Models Conscience Being Formed	Image of Self Independence Experimentation with Values System Conscience Tested

The idea here is that as we progress in the development of our lives, we interact with both the masculine and feminine representatives of the one who created us. We learn of Him through our experience of dependency on them. Then, as we move into the stage of life where values are formed, we acquire the maturity necessary for us to learn interdependency. Finally, we enter the stage where we begin testing our values. In this stage, we learn to relate to Him directly, in our own responsible manner, becoming increasingly independent of his representatives.

When I look at this, I realize how blessed I was to be

raised by the same two role models for all of my development. My parents were by no means perfect and there have been several issues that I was determined as I became a parent that I would do differently. But my parents were consistent and they were there.

Divorce, the death of one or both parents, infidelity, and any of a myriad of events that disrupt and distort the interaction between our mother and father can adversely affect our sexual identity. The early years and then the time of values formation will temper or incline our sexual experimentation.

Now I have known individuals who have come from broken homes who turned out fine, so I am not saying that everyone who encounters a disruption in the formulation of ones identity as a sexual being will be messed up sexually. I am saying that they will have issues that need to be dealt with. God designed the pattern for our development and any deviation from His design is risky at best.

I know I have been verbose in relating this section, but I feel it is of the utmost importance to understand how we relate to God, parents, siblings, mates, children, and those around us.

Let's examine how parents help shape the sexual identity of a child during the childhood years, we come to the role values have in the process.

"The Roxy Art Theatre and the Bible"

You will need very little coaching in order to remember most of the events that played a role in formulating your sexual identity. I'd like to tell you about some of the events that shaped my view of sex.

Sometime in my childhood I remember seeing an advertisement for the movies shown at the Roxy Art Theatre. I innocently asked my parents in the presence of some relatives if we could go to the show and showed them the ad in the paper. My dad and uncle started laughing and said something along the line of, "Yeah girls, let's go see one of these movies." My mom and aunt blushed and told them to shut up. I didn't understand and the response I was given was by my mom. She said, "No! Those kinds of movies are not for little boys; they're for dirty old men." I suppose that last part was a stab at my dad who thought the whole thing was rather funny. It must have gotten my mom thinking because a few days later she called me into the living room. I came in and noticed that she was reading her bible. She called me over and said, "I have something for you to read." She then handed me the bible and told me to read the portion she had marked. It was the words of Jesus in the gospels telling a group that adulterers and fornicators would burn in the fire of hell. I read it and looked at her somewhat confused. She responded that sex was for marriage and I could go to hell for messing around with girls. As far as she was concerned, that was the end of the subject!

When I look back, the interaction I observed between my parents as it relates to romance was a positive one. They kept sexual conversations, touches, and related acts behind closed doors, while in front of us they showed affection with hugs, kisses and tenderness. In public and in front of us my dad was a gentleman and my mom a lady. Therefore it is easy for me to see that the good I exhibited toward the opposite sex was founded in the values they taught through their actions. However, as the Roxy and the Bible illustrates, we are always teaching our children our values and we really have no idea which ones stick or make the biggest impression.

What this encounter did was stir my curiosity and, unfortunately, I found satisfaction to my inquisitive nature in pornography. While my parents set a good example and model for proper interaction outside the bedroom, pornography set the tone for what goes on behind closed doors and my attitudes about sexual conduct were formed with the help of pornography.

As a young father I looked back on the struggle I had changing my conscience from one that was perverted to one with a proper understanding of sex. I determined to help my children avoid this duplicity. It is important to note that at the time of this determination I was clueless as to how to go about it. This book is not a "How To" manual about sex. I intend for it to be something of a guide for development of the whole person. However some instructions are needed.

First of all, PRAY! Earlier in this book I discussed praying the word of God as one of the cleansing activities for the mind and referenced the appendix on prayers. I want to point you to the prayers found in Ephesians and Colossians. Turn to them and use them specifically for you and your mate and for your children and their future mates. When Cathy and I found out we were going to be parents I began praying to experience the hope of God's calling as a father to this child. Likewise I asked concerning my calling as a father in law to the child's future mate. With this in mind I prayed for this mate's parents as well. I included the riches of Christ's inheritance and the available power of the Holy Spirit for each one.

The Colossian prayer was for specific subjects. Take time before you go any further to examine these prayers if you have not done so. Also, it helps with both cleansing and preparation for child rearing to write the prayer out putting in specific names and praying them out loud when possible. I have a coffee mug with my granddaughter's picture on it and pray for her each morning using it as a reminder.

Secondly, teach them what to expect as proper treatment from the opposite sex. If what our children observe in our treatment of each other as mates finds support in our instructions and in turn develops the foundation in their sexual self image, then how we treat them reinforces that identity and gives its first proving ground for personal experience. Not sexual experience, but simply relating to the opposite sex.

Let's cover the spectrum of human interaction through the five senses.

Sight: Be careful concerning personal privacy when it comes to nudity. Neither you nor your children need to have the visual image in their memory of anyone's nudity. While it may be a necessity when they are in the dependent stage, once they are able to take care of themselves you need to allow them their privacy. Also if viewing of them becomes a necessity because of health reasons it needs to be male to male and female to female. If you have not viewed your child in such a manner then there are no pictures in the mind for the enemy to use against you. If an improper mindset concerning sex has never been a problem you may think these warnings are unnecessary. However, if your background includes sexual impurity of any kind, then I hope you understand the concern and the need for these cautions.

Be careful how you touch each other in view of your children as they mimic what they see. I made mention of this earlier when discussing the way my parents treated each other in front of my siblings and me.

Touch and Hearing: As parents we kiss, hug, and touch our children affectionately and rightly so. What I don't want is for someone to take what I am expressing here to the extreme and completely fail to be affectionate in front of their children or with them. What made me realize this void in my own life was a very important event, my ordination into the ministry. I was ordained at twenty-three and the thing that stood out the most that day had nothing to do with the ordination.

Without my knowledge my pastor had asked my father to present the ordination papers to me at the end of the service. So as I was standing with the pastor at the end of the service he received the documents from the ordination counsel and then announced that my father was going to come forward and present the papers to me. My dad came forward, took the documents, handed them to me, hugged me, whispering in my ear that he was proud of me and said, "I love you". Tears form in my eyes as I write this even though I have shared it many times. It was this event that caused me to determine that my children would not have a day pass without a touch, a kiss, and the words "I love you".

My dad was not one to show affection to us children. Hearing me mention this one day my mom defended him by saying that when we were small he held, hugged, and kissed us all the time, but as we grew he got away from it. Even as unaccustomed as we are in our culture for men and their sons to embrace and show affection in public, I think it is a great legacy to pass on to them. Pass it on.

"Too few men in our day can distinguish between intimate and sexual touching."

Our failure to communicate the subject of intimacy in our homes and churches facilitates the need to cover it in a book, rather than leaving it to our public school system. Because of the many requests from audiences for follow up information every time I speak in a church, school, or at a conference, I became convinced I needed to include it here.

Realizing my inability to distinguish and exhibit proper behavior drove me to learn the right way. I will forever be grateful to Christian authors such as James Dobson, Tim and Beverly LaHaye, Donald Joy, Gary Chapman, and many others that produced informative, accurate and above all, Godly books and audio products. I estimated at one point that I had read close to a hundred books on the subject of marriage, sex and parenting. Having said this, if you were to ask me which item was of the most assistance concerning the subject of intimacy, I would recommend Donald Joy's work titled, "Bonding" and "Rebonding".

<u>Smell and Taste:</u> These two senses are more of a support group for the first three. However, the memories they evoke are as real and can be a tool the enemy uses in his attempt to control our minds. One of the earliest images I have is brought to mind by the smell of a bakery. For a brief period of time my dad got his hair cut at a barber shop that was next to a donut shop. I can close my eyes and see myself as a four or five year old standing with my nose pressed to the storefront window, admiring the glazed donuts. That image comes to mind anytime I go near a bakery.

In summary, memories are made by passing through our conscious mind via our five senses. These same senses then become the vehicles by which memories are brought up from our sub-conscious mind back to a conscious awareness.

In review of this developmental stage, I conclude with this statement: "The experimentation we go through in connection with the values we have been taught will formulate our self-image which in turn will control our behavior. The kind of person we will exhibit through our character is the person that has been forged into our subconscious memory."

Most of our waking hours are engaged with unconscious reactions to our current situation rather than calculated responses. The majority of our daily activity comes from the images deep within the recesses of our subconscious mind. If we are not happy with how we act then the subconscious mind is where we need to initiate change. Change at this level requires reconstruction. Anyone in construction will tell you that remodeling is more expensive and takes longer than new construction.

While studying for my contractor's license I discovered that concrete goes through a curing process for over a hundred years, even though within a few hours it may hold firm consistency and appear to be completely hardened. With this in mind let's imagine that we are going to pour a sidewalk in front of your house. First we will lay down the form boards. These forms will determine the shape and size of our walk. Next, having prepared the contours of our walk we pour in the concrete mix. Now that we have the mix in place we have a brief amount of time in which we can change the placement of the concrete and then trowel the finish on the surface.

Our minds follow a close parallel to this process. The forms of the content of our mind are laid out by our parents in the first stage of our development. Remember that upwards of eighty-five percent of our personality is shaped during these first few years. Balance is achieved by bouncing back and forth between masculine and feminine interaction during these early years. Imagine what can happen if you remove one side of your sidewalk forms. You will not have much of a sidewalk with only one form. In addition, should you remove one side too quickly before the mix had ample time to set, the result could be disastrous.

Our relative sense of security and stability will shape the content that fills the forms of our thinking process. Just as the formboards for our sidewalk limits the amount of concrete we will need, so the form of our personality will determine the content of our values. The content of these values will then determine how the individual fares in the next stage. With concrete, the wrong mix of ingredients can create difficulties in the finishing process and make for a poor sidewalk. Likewise, the wrong values given to us in the second stage will create difficulties in the third stage, the stage where we test these values.

Finally we put the trowel of experimentation in the adult world to the values we have received and the world views the results. We now are birthing our reputation. I heard someone say once, "Reputation is what people think is true of you and character is what your family knows to be true. If the process of your development has been true to God's design then reputation and character should be identical. I believe that only we know if this is true about ourselves.

If your reputation and your character are not the same you have some work to do. Or I should say the Spirit has work to do in you. And, if you are His, He will work on you!

SECTION THREE
COMBINING LAKE MIND AND THE TIMELINE

The purpose of this chapter will be to combine the Lake Mind illustration with the Timeline of Development to give us a tool that will allow you to take back what was stolen from you by the enemy. This statement raises the question, "What has been stolen from me?" What was stolen from you is the opportunity to be who God has called you to be. The specific answer is one that only God can answer and you are the only one who can receive it.

"He said good things about you before the foundation of the world."

It is comforting to know that the condition I found myself in before being born again is not what the Father intended. Not only that, but the conflict and torment I went through those first few years were not of His design. I know this because the bible teaches that He spoke my name before even the world was brought into existence. Imagine that! The voice that caused creation to come into existence took time within the Godhead to verbalize the details of my being. Read the following excerpt from scripture.

Blessed be the God and Father of our Lord Jesus Christ, who has blessed us with all spiritual blessings in heavenly places in Christ: According as he has chosen us in him before the foundation of the world, that we should be holy and without blame before him in love: Having predestined us unto the adoption of children by Jesus Christ to himself, according to the good pleasure of his will; to the praise of the glory of his grace. Ephesians 1:3-6

Several words stand out in this passage. The first to grab my attention is the word *blessed.* The root word for blessed is the Greek word *logos.* Within the context of this passage, it means "to speak well of". It is in what is called the *aorist* tense in Greek. This tense does not have a connection to time in and of itself. Our language has but three tenses and they relate to the time of action; past, present, and future. Greek on the other hand has five base tenses and they relate to the type of action rather than the time. When a word does not have a time indicator as a prefix or suffix then it gains a reference to time from the context. A word in the aorist tense gives an indication of action that is not limited to a specific time or activity. The action of the aorist tense is called 'punctilious'. This means it is a 'on the spot' event.

The reason I can state that it was not God's design that I should go through torment during the first years of my conversion is found in the second use of the word *blessed* in verse 3. Paul informs us that God has blessed us at a point in time with every spiritual blessing in heavenly places in Christ. Verse 4 gives us the context of time: *"Just as He chose us in Him before the foundation of the world".* I shall never forget the first time I realized what Paul was saying. I got goose bumps (Holy Ghost Bumps as a friend of mine calls them). The word blessed means that God literally spoke my name and said good things about me. The voice that spoke creation into being rang out in the presence of the angels and described my existence and this took place before he created the world. Think about if for a moment, you were in design before the order of the cosmos was established. This means that the world was created as a support for God's image bearer. We are not a creative after thought designed to take care of the earth.

Somehow the fall fits into His plan. One of the mysteries theologians wrestle with is where evil came from. For those who find answers in a sovereign existence, the question is supralapsarian or infralapsarian. I don't think you will find these words in Webster's so let me offer a brief definition.

Lapsarian has to do with the introduction of sin into the created order. Supralapsarian asks the question, "How can a perfect God create a man with the capacity to sin?" Infralapsarian asks, "If man was made in innocence and perfection how could he sin?" I don't believe either of these questions will be answered this side of heaven. The question is and will remain a mystery unless God gives us the answer when we stand before Him. Somehow I don't believe it will matter at that point. Therefore I know that regardless of how sin entered the scene, and the fall took place, God has loftier and grander designs for us.

When I came to an understanding of this truth the image in my mind of who I was changed. I understood what Paul was saying and I began to pray the following;

Lord, I agree today with all that you have said about me since before the world began. Everything that you said about me I accept and ask that you bring it into this present reality. Also that which is in me that does not agree with what you have spoken concerning me I confess and desire that it be removed. I added this to the prayer of chapter 1:15-23.

THE TIMELINE IN REVERSE

Understand that the cleansing of the mind is only the first step in restoration of the mind. The next step is discovering who we are in Christ. What I suggest next is for you to trace back through the timeline of your developmental process. As the days pass and you begin discovering your identity, specific memories will surface that have left a negative impact on your self-image.

For example, take the trait of truthfulness. There is no doubt that your identity in Christ would have you to be truthful. The Spirit will make this clear the next time you are deceptive and will lead you to confess your deceitfulness as sin, ask for cleansing, and lead you to commit to being truthful. In accord with the process illustrated in Lake Mind, your thinking will become clearer and you will see deeper into your memory. The exercise I recommend next will help you understand the nature and extent of the issues you need to deal with in this area.

Someplace in a journal, diary, or even on one of those blank pages in your bible draw a line across the page putting your birth date to the left and your present age on the far right. Next along the line spacing as best you can place the following events with the age above them.

D.O.B / Crisis of values / Puberty / Conversion / Loss of innocence / Tragic event / Age /

I recommend that you use symbols or initials for the information you will put on this line for your own privacy and protection. Much of what you are going to place on this line is private and does not need to be revealed to anyone. I have pretty much opened the book of my life as I have shared my testimony and related these truths to others but, while I have shared what I was prior to my conversion, I have shared very few details of what I did. For example, you know that I was hooked on pornography but not what that addiction caused me to do. The degree to which anyone listening to my testimony has had involvement gives him all the information they need to relate. To give details of personal acts only paints a false image of who I am. God says that I am holy, sanctified, and without blemish. These are the things God has declared me to be in response to my declaration of faith in His Son. The Bible says God cannot lie. Therefore the truth is this...I am who God says I am; I am not what my sin (past, present or future) may represent me to be.

On the timeline, place the age you became a Christian. I do this by drawing a cross and putting "71" above it. Using events from my life as an example, a sample timeline would look similar to this:

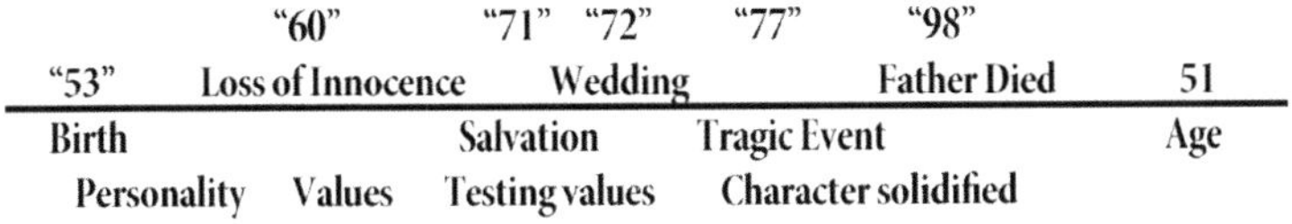

"60" "71" "72" "77" "98"

"53" Loss of Innocence Wedding Father Died 51

Birth Salvation Tragic Event Age

Personality Values Testing values Character solidified

I have put the distinctions from the development line as a reminder of the stage of development I was going through when the event took place.

The Event of the Cross

The developmental stage you were in during the occurrence of each event will help in determining how much effort will have to be exerted in order for you to experience genuine change. The conversion experience is a good example.

My conversion took place about the time I was graduating from high school in "71". I was at the end of my experimentation with my assumed values.

When I was growing up we rarely went to church, so the cross had little influence during the development of my personality. Therefore as I entered the stage where my basic values were developed, my conscience was formed without the influence of the Holy Spirit through God's word. There was only the influence of the morals my mother displayed. However, since I was a boy, the influence of my father, uncles, cousins, and brother had a greater and weightier impression. Because of that, I came out of the values development stage determined to do things their way. I knew what I wanted to experience was wrong but the odds were stacked against me. How much different would that have been had I been taught the word of God and had godly men in my life whom I could look up to? I suspect that some of my relatives will read this and rise in defense. I don't write this to offend, but the truth is those who stood for God in my extended family were ridiculed and made fun of by those I looked up to and respected.

What all this means is that I had to renounce much of what I experimented with, reprogram much of my values, and work on my character once I became a Christian. I must admit that I did not like who I was in my early twenties. Much of that was because of the frustration that came from learning in my head from the word who I was supposed to be and yet having a subconscious mind that reacted with memories from seventeen years of development without the influence of God's Word.

My friends at church kept telling me I was a new creature in Christ and that if I continued in sin it was because I wanted to. They were partly right. Unconsciously my actions were driven by the habits gained over the years. Yet consciously I despised myself and wanted to change. I just didn't know how. That is why I'm writing this book.

Hopefully you see why I am having you go through this exercise. Knowing the truth about who you are will give you the freedom to be who you were designed to be. It may be that the freedom you begin to experience is that of patience with yourself as you realize that you have a lot of work ahead of you.

Allow me to interject at this point a word of concern. If your cross is to the far left of your timeline and your parents raised you under the influence of the cross, then you may tend to be impatient with those whose background is similar to mine. I cannot count the number of times I have heard criticism of my failures when what was needed was acceptance and help. I'm afraid that most of those who have walked this path have given up long before they had time to go through a transformation that only comes by the power of God.

Puberty and Loss of Innocence

The next two items to be placed on the line are puberty and what I call the loss of innocence. Puberty is the time of our passage from childhood into young adulthood. Loss of innocence occurs at a point in time when we come upon the knowledge of human sexuality.

The term 'loss of innocence' should not be taken in a negative manner although it may be a traumatic time. The relationship between puberty and the loss of innocence can be crucial to a healthy sexual self-image. Before we can see how this relationship can be helpful or damaging we need to understand what happens during puberty.

Estrogen

Estrogen is a female hormone. It is one of the substances

that the mother's body uses in the development of a female fetus. Once the baby has become fully formed and subsequently delivered it remains dormant. As the female child grows, except for the way we dress her and how she may wear her hair, her shape and features are not much different than those of a male child.

Then puberty begins around ten to twelve years of age and estrogen becomes active once again, causing her to blossom into a young woman. Her menstrual cycle begins, which is usually the first sign that puberty is about to go into full swing. Body hair grows and she adds curves to a once boy-like body shape.

Androgen

Androgen is the male hormone. Females have this hormone in order for them to bear sons. All fetuses are female when they are first formed. Then in the tenth to thirteenth week of gestation if the chromosome determines that this one is to be a male, the mother's body will inject androgen into the right side of the brain. This causes a shrinking of the right side of the brain, leading some to believe that all men are born brain damaged. Seriously though, it is believed that this causes an interruption in the communication of the two hemispheres of the brain, causing men to think like an old key punch calculator where you punch in the numbers and pull a lever for the total. Women, who have not experienced this interruption, act like a computer with intuitive calculations and output. The physical effect at this time is in the changes that take place in the genitals. Once this happens, the fetuses sex organs are transformed into male genitals. Like estrogen in the female, androgen has an active role while the male is in the womb and then remains dormant until puberty. Usually at a little later age than the female, puberty stirs up this hormone and the male will experience a growth spurt, along with facial and body hair. His voice will deepen and he will pick up muscle mass.

I failed to give a disclaimer when I began this section so I do so now. I am not a biologist. I took science in school, but most of what I have learned has come from self study, so realize that much of what I am relating here are generalizations and take them as such. My intent is not to educate about human development, but to give enough background to enable you to understand the relationship of our sexual identity to our experience.

Loss of Innocence

Until they come to the stark reality of what human sexuality entails, members of both sexes have a mindset of innocence toward themselves and each other. This innocence allows us to grow physically, emotionally, and mentally without the interplay and competition of sexual conduct. The foundation to all relationships is the need for companionship. The dormancy of our hormones during our childhood years provides not only the time for development of values, but also a time for establishing relationships without the pressure that comes with sexual activity. This time of innocence lays the foundation for the later complex interaction that comes from adding sexual needs and gratification to those of companionship. You may want to see the work I have on the four stages of a relationship, which I call The Cycle of Love, to get a better understanding about the connection between companionship and sex.

The facts about human sexuality incite selfishness for personal gratification in both sexes that is not known before this awareness comes into play. While this selfishness is more pronounced in the male it exists in the female as well. I call this a loss of innocence, but I don't consider this necessarily a bad thing. James Dobson states that when a child experiences this loss of innocence prior to puberty, it locks him or her into maturity at this level. Thus a nine year old boy who experiences a sexual encounter will tend to treat subsequent sexual partners as a nine year old. Shortly after hearing Dr. Dobson relate this information, I began counseling a woman at our church whose life verified the truth of it. This female came to me after hearing me speak about relationships at a singles conference.

She was a very successful forty-year old executive with a major insurance underwriter. She looked and acted the role exquisitely. I had observed her for several months after she joined the singles group at church, learned of her status, and was impressed with her stature. Yet, in the midst of all this, her choice in men was puzzling. Despite her attractiveness, job status, and otherwise sophisticated demeanor, her choice of male companions was puzzling. She attended a singles conference where I was teaching the contents of this work and requested an appointment.

I began her timeline in the first session after hearing the woes of this latest failed relationship. When we came to puberty and the loss of innocence her eyes began to tear up. During my explanation of what happens to us when loss of innocence happens prior to puberty the tears became sobs and she lost all composure. I quietly began to pray for her and allowed her to calm down. Gently I began to discuss how I had been amazed by her choice in men given her social status and professionalism. She interrupted me and declared, "You don't know the half of it!"

I hope I hid my shock as she related her numerous failed marriages and subsequent affairs. I realized that this was a tale of torment in which she could not help herself, so I began the timeline in reverse starting with this current relationship and we began the process of Lake Mind by writing down the beginning and ending of each relationship she experienced. I quickly saw a pattern, realized how immature she was in each encounter and jumped back to puberty.

She entered womanhood at a normal age of twelve and related little out of the ordinary as to her development. Then, as I began to inquire concerning her loss of innocence, she began to tear up again. She maintained her composure as she told me of a relative's attention and subsequent sexual abuse that continued for several years. After talking with her about the guilt and shame this event caused, she began to understand that it was not her fault. We discussed how this guilt and shame caused her to feel unworthy as a woman and was influencing her choice in men. We spent the next hour in a study of what the Bible teaches about guilt and forgiveness and ended with a confessional prayer renouncing this grievous act against her. Part of our prayer centered on asking God to heal her emotions. We also requested an unlocking of her maturity when dealing with men. This lady soon after left our church where she had so much negative history. While attending another, she met a man much more suited to her socially, married him, started a family and started living the life that was robbed from her for over thirty years.

Her timeline looked like this:

"58" "60" "68" "72" "77"

"50" T LOI Marriage/Divorce 3X 40

Birth Personality Values Testing values Character solidified Age

On the positive side

As detrimental as the loss of innocence can be when happening before puberty it is not a sign that all is lost. We are resilient creatures and with the help of God can overcome incredible obstacles. As the saying goes though, "An ounce of prevention is worth a pound of cure." It is imperative that we as parents and citizens take whatever measures are necessary to help our children experience puberty and the loss of innocence within the context of proper timing and framework.

As parents we control the environment where situations can arise that would be detrimental in our child's development. Without becoming isolationist by joining a commune or locking our child in a closet we must monitor all the activities and events that pose a danger to them. This is a daunting task that requires divine assistance. How can we even begin to assume that we can raise our children without God's hand involved on a daily basis? Listen to the Psalmist David;

Unless the Lord build the house, they labor in vain who build it; Unless the Lord guard the city, the watchman stays awake in vain. It is vain for you to rise up early, to sit up late, to eat the bread of sorrows; for so He gives His beloved sleep. Behold, children are a heritage from the Lord, the fruit of the womb is a reward. Like arrows in the hand of a warrior, so are the children of one's youth. Happy is the man who has his quiver full of them; they shall not be ashamed, but shall speak with their enemies in the gate.

To me the word *vain* stands out. For us to attempt to raise our children without the assistance and help of the Lord is futile.

As citizens we need to influence our culture in a positive manner as well. Sex education does not belong in the public schools. Yet our failure to influence and control the availability of sexually focused material keeps pressing the school systems to step in.

The tasks we face deserve more attention than I can give within the scope of this book. Therefore I beg you to dig, investigate and become involved in both the development of your children and the changing of our culture.

"Death and Divorce"

As I go through this material I find it difficult at best to determine which event is the most influential in our development. No two people are affected the same. While a late introduction to the cross may cripple one, it is a premature loss of innocence that has devastated another. So when we move into our next subject I am not lowering it on the scale of influence by making it third or fourth. It's just that in writing to a predominately Christian audience the cross and its effect will be universal. Likewise we are all sexual beings and sexuality is all encompassing. Death and divorce might be two events that someone reading this material may not have encountered with someone close and influential.

In relating someone's death or divorce to our timeline we are investigating the disruption of the nest where our development takes place. While the cross and sexuality are both related to our internal and personal development, death and divorce relate to the environment of our development.

"With the death of a parent one of our brackets is gone."

Earlier we saw that our parents are the brackets that we bounce back and forth between. We saw how our image of God as well as our masculine and feminine traits found models as we interacted with our parents while growing up. Also this bracketing established our idea of 'roles' during the values stage. And they became the safety net that released us into adulthood as we experimented with these values, established our role and manifested our sexual identity.

Understanding the above the question arises, "What happens when a parent dies before the child becomes an adult?"

The answer can be as simple as, "When my father died we moved in with my mom's folks and my grandfather assumed the masculine role model." Or it can be as complex as, "My father died when I was one. I was the baby of four children and the only boy. I grew up playing with dolls with my sisters and I just prefer feminine things." That's a broad overview of the spectrum, from role model replacement to total absence of one, with a resultant imbalance in sexual identity.

"Role Model Replacement"

For most of us, our families are extended enough for there to be a grandparent, aunt or uncle, or older brother or sister to step in the gap if a parent dies. This is not always the case, though. In the event there is not someone in the family to fulfill the role, we should first look within the church for assistance. If that fails, then secular organizations that check out as being trustworthy may fill the need. The word trustworthy is the key. There are those in every arena that will take advantage of our children, so be sure the one you ask for assistance is worthy of the responsibility you're asking them to assume. Also, don't demand perfection. The one who died was not perfect; his or her replacement won't be either.

Realize that something will fill the void left when a parent passes. Do not fail to pay attention to your child's need for a role model. Divorce can be as traumatic as death in its effect. Sometimes it is even more difficult for a child to handle than if a parent dies. With the death of a parent we recognize that something bigger than us is at work. I have heard a parent explain how 'Daddy went to be with Jesus' or some other reason being given for his no longer being around. With divorce the parent is not around except for visitation weekends or other special events. For a small child who grows up with this arrangement it may seem the norm. That however does not make it less detrimental for the child. It is possible for two adults to arrange events to lessen divorce's effect, but it will have an effect. I don't intend this as a guilt trip, but the truth is the truth and empathy for those experiencing divorce notwithstanding, it needs to be told. Divorce is devastating to a child! For a child going through the stage of values development it can disrupt their conscience and influence their experimentation stage.

I often begin a conference on relationships with the statement, "The only way to avoid getting a divorce is to not have it as an option." If, when going into a relationship, you have the option of walking away when things get tough, you will walk away sooner or later. I promise you in relationships things will get tough! And when a child grows up experiencing the divorce of his or her parents they are more likely to enter into a relationship with the option of bowing out when things get tough.

I will never forget the first time I heard the word divorce. I was no more than seven or eight years old. We were at my grandparent's home in rural Georgia on a Sunday afternoon. As was the custom after the noon meal the women gathered on the back porch and discussed family. I was not allowed there because there was always someone nursing a baby and that was no place for little boys. The men congregated on the front porch and discussed the Viet Nam war. Again little boys didn't need to be around. You however know the curiosity little boys have when they are denied something, so I cleverly went under the raised floor of the old farm house and would crawl from front to back listening in on the conversations.

When the women on the back porch would lower their voice it usually indicated that the subject was juicy or taboo. On one such occasion I overheard them discuss a couple that had not gathered with our families for several weeks. The reason given for their absence was their impending divorce. It was not until later in the week that I mustered up the courage to ask my mother what a divorce was. Her answered shocked me.

We are talking about the early 1960'ss. By the time I was in my teens our culture was viewing what was called "Break-through TV" with programs about divorce, pre-marital sex, abortion, homosexuality, and other progressive lifestyles. Now we live with the results of such cultural enlightenment. We are actually having to define what a marriage is and are seeing a movement to make such a definition a constitutional amendment. In my hometown of Jacksonville, Florida the divorce rate was 76% in 1995. In the church it is now over 50%. I can name only a few of my peers who have not had their homes touched by divorce. We truly have come a long way baby. Unfortunately, the wrong way!

What are we to do? Two things can be done about our dilemma. First, inasmuch as it is up to you, determine to stay married. Marriage is the first institution set up by God to control and direct the lives of His creatures. If it is an entity in and of itself, then your sticking it out will strengthen it while your divorce will help continue its demise.

Second, if you have been through a divorce, seek help. Strive for restoration if possible and rehabilitation if reconciliation is not available. I say available rather than optional because love is a matter of choice. Often in the counseling office someone laments about not being in love any longer. To which I respond with, "When did you decide to stop loving your mate?" This response is usually met by, "Oh I didn't choose, I just lost all feeling for them." To which I reply, "Yes, you did choose. There was a time after you met when you decided that you wanted to be with him or her. That choice was the foundation for your love...not your feelings. Feelings come and go in relationships. It's the choice to stay or leave that determines love. So again I ask, when did you decide?"

Those of you who have experienced divorce (or have a loved one within its clutches) may think I sound rather cold and calculating. Just the opposite is true. I am ready to help those who have been ravaged by divorce, but I must be honest. Divorce is devastating to our lives and especially to our development. If we expect to see our culture turn around morally, we must begin with the body of Christ and with the current laxness of conscience toward marriage.

I was ordained as a deacon at twenty one years of age and was confused when several seemingly qualified men were passed over because of a divorce in their past. Two of these men were not at fault and could not help their marital circumstances. Yet my pastor stood firm and it took both these men discussing my need to move forward before I allowed my ordination to take place. Still I felt the church was passing an opportunity by, in not ordaining these men. Times have changed. Such a mindset today would prevent most churches from ordaining anyone. I recently learned that one of the above mentioned men is now the chairman of deacons at this same church (New pastor; new mindset).

This fact bears out the truth that we adjust to our environment. You can decide for yourself whether or not you think this is good. It is a fact we live with nonetheless.

If you are dealing with a divorce, follow the process prescribed before. Acknowledge the sin involved in causing the divorce, then pray for cleansing and healing. In your praying, do the same for those involved and ask for things to be set in the order of God's declaration concerning their lives. Where necessary, seek forgiveness and restoration. If remarriage is a possibility, be sure to obtain wise counsel before moving forward. Realize that we all make our own choices and while we may be able to change the direction of our own lives, we cannot control the choices of others.

> *"God grant us the serenity*
> *to accept the things we cannot change,*
> *courage to change the things we can,*
> *and wisdom to know the difference."*

Know this: as devastating as a death or divorce may have been in your development, God's grace and mercy are greater. You cannot change what you experienced because of it, but you do not have to continue to live under their influence in the future. Choose to overcome. The God of all mercies and grace is waiting for the invitation to go to work. Remember the story of the prodigal son. Your heavenly father is watching the road, ready to run and meet you and restore you to the position that has been yours all along.

Tragedy or Crisis

The final event(s) to place on your timeline should be traumatic events that we call tragedies or crises. For our purposes, a tragedy is defined as an event that affects you with devastating results. It may have to do with your health (physical or mental), finances, loss of a job, or relationship. These events are usually beyond our control. A crisis may be just as traumatic. The difference lies with the demand of action on our part. In other words, a crisis is a tragedy that puts us in a position of having to make a decision. And such decisions create difficulties.

"The fall was a tragedy that developed into a series of crises."

Less than a year before writing this book I experienced an event that is a perfect example of the kind of event I am referencing. At 4:30 in the afternoon on September the tenth, I was climbing a girder truss to connect a crane's hook onto a roof truss that we needed to change. Some thirty feet into my ascent, I stepped onto a brace, it gave way, and I tumbled all the way to the concrete floor below. I was treated to a LifeFlight ride to Shand's Trauma Center in Jacksonville and a ninety day stay flat on my back while my broken and crushed bones healed.

Obviously I survived, but this tragic fall soon developed into a crisis. The first crisis was physical in nature. At the time of this writing I am still going through rehabilitation and am facing a hip replacement sometime in the near future. Along with the difficulty of learning to walk again and regain control of simple bodily functions, I faced the crisis of no longer being able to work. So the next crisis was financial. While I was covered by workers compensation, which covered my medical expenses, my absence from the day to day operations soon put us in red financially.

My wife and son were the next ones affected. My wife not only became my nurse, but also the business manager of our company. These new roles were added to the duties she already had of managing our household and babysitting our two year old granddaughter. My son, who lives over a hundred and fifty miles north of us and has his own construction company, spent several days a week for several months overseeing the houses my company was constructing. You can easily see how a fall that was a tragedy developed into a series of crises that affected my entire family.

The importance of placing tragedies or crises on the timeline helps in sorting out their effects—past events may help reveal present difficulties. A lot of phobias can often be traced back to a traumatic event and the discovery of the relationship between the present and the past can bring freedom from the phobia and its resulting consequences.

I remember a seminar leader relating such an event from his life. He would be driving down the highway and for no apparent reason he would suddenly jerk the steering wheel to the right, sometimes driving off the highway. It scared him to say the least and he sought professional help. He was informed that he was having some kind of an anniversary reaction. His counselor advised him to stop and check his surroundings the next time it happened. Several days later it happened again, so he pulled off the road, looked around and checked his rear view mirror. When he looked in the mirror, he saw the taillights of a1950 Mercury that a car buff had recently restored and occasionally drove in the area. Immediately he recognized the source of his problem. The seminar leader remembered that he had had a head on collision—with a 1950 Mercury—nearly thirty years earlier and then recalled that the last thing he did trying to avoid the collision was jerk the steering wheel to the right. He related that, after recognizing the source of the reaction, it was no longer a problem.

In summation:

- Begin to pray the prayer of Paul in Ephesians 1 by personalizing the entire chapter. Do this daily, agreeing with everything that God has said about you. Asking for recognition of everything that is a part of you that conflicts with your God-given calling, then confess it for cleansing.

- During devotions, read the Psalms, Ephesians, and Romans. The Psalms will give you additional prayers to help in the mental release of memories that haunt you. Ephesians will give you practical reminders of how to do your part in the sanctification process. Romans will begin to give you a proper understanding of who God is as well as what He has done for you and is doing in you.
- Don't get locked into a ritual with the timeline, it is just a visual tool to help you apply the truth of God's Word to your life.

Most important of all remember this: God is faithful. Paul told Timothy that even when we are faithless, He remains faithful for He cannot deny Himself. I do not discount instantaneous transformations. I believe that God sets people free from addictions and habits, but I believe they are the exception, not the rule. For most of us God causes us to develop disciplines for dealing with our past. That does not mean that He is not at work in us all the time. You can follow the tools I have presented here or any other number of helpful tools that are available, but if God is not at work in you they will be futile.

A NEW MINDSET

"Who I am is often confused by what I've done."

I encourage you to undertake going through this exercise even if you are not currently facing any dire circumstance. The only thing you will lose may be the one thing keeping you from realization of who you are in Christ. I worked through the difficulties of fleshly desires and my defeat at their every beckoning with the use of this tool. Yet in the years between those early victories and my current situation I have continued to benefit from this exercise. We must realize that no matter how far removed we may be from the domination of certain fleshly attacks we are not above temptation and failure. Also the enemy is crafty and will change tactics, offering those same defeated habits in a different way.

Therefore I challenge you to stay alert, for as Peter states, *"Be sober, be vigilant, because your adversary the devil walks about like a roaring lion, seeking whom he may devour. Resist him steadfast in the faith, knowing that the same sufferings are experienced by your brotherhood in the world." I Peter 5:8&9*

Perhaps the single greatest benefit I received with this exercise through the years has come with the realization that who I am is often confused by what I've done. This tool has helped me through confession and cleansing to separate the two. I am who God says I am, not what my habits, vices, and character flaws might indicate. If this sounds confusing or reeks of false piety I apologize. My intention is not to confuse or sound hypocritical. Nor do I seek to be labeled heretical. I know as long as we remain in this body of death we will never become sinless, but we should be on a path of growth where we sin less with each passing day. And yet it seems each time I overcome a particular sin or fault another rises to the top. I am not new in such a realization. Because this is our common dilemma, many have come to the conclusion that we are, "Just sinners saved by the grace".

The primary problem with such a self-evaluation is that it predisposes us to a life of failure. If I walk through the course of my life telling myself I am just a sinner that has experienced salvation I am accepting this image of myself as the excuse for continuing in sin. I walk along and sin and immediately coupled with my guilty conscience and the accusation of my enemy is my defense that it is to be expected from one who is 'just a sinner'.

"What appears as true may not be the truth"

The difficulty I find with our popular saying is the fact that what appears to be true may not be the truth. What do I mean? Have I lost my mind? Have I finally proven my madness? Think with me for a moment. How often do we read in the scripture that we are called things and we scoff at the statements in our mind? The bible calls us saints, holy ones, blameless, righteous, priest…just to list a few of the titles we are to signify with our lives. Yet how many of us perform a deed that would identify with such a title and think to ourselves, "Yep, that's right, after all I am the righteousness of Christ, called to good works!"

You may be accusing me of being sarcastic or even sacrilegious, but before you label me as such think about it. If sinning makes me a sinner, then wouldn't performing righteous acts make me righteous? You know as well as I that such a thought concerning righteousness flies in the face of what we know concerning our standing with God. I am made righteous by the transference of my sin to the cross. That's the truth. My righteous acts cannot make me righteous. It is likewise the truth that sinful acts on my part cannot undo or negate my having been made the righteousness of God in Christ. Listen to Paul;

"For he made Him who knew no sin to be sin for us, that we might become the righteousness of God in Him." II Corinthians 5:21

Therefore, I must conclude that what appears to be true may not be the truth. Jesus tells us in the gospel of John 8:32 *"And you shall know the truth and the truth shall make you free."* He did not say things that are true bring freedom. The distinction between things being true and that which is the truth, can find no better example than that of our righteousness. The truth is we are righteous. Yet it is true that we act at times as if we are not.

Now I do not propose to solve this seemingly apparent contradiction. This paradox has perplexed Christians since the time of the early church. Listen to Paul:

"For we know that the law is spiritual, but I am carnal, sold under sin. For what I am doing , I do not understand. For what I will to do, that I do not practice; but what I hate that I do. If then, I do what I will not to do, I agree with the law that it is good. But now, it is no longer I who do it, but sin that dwells in me. For I know that in me (that is in my flesh) nothing good dwells; for to will is present with me, but how to perform what is good I do not find. For the good that I will to do, I do not do; but the evil I will not to do, that I practice. Now if I do what I will not to do, it is no longer I who do it, but sin that dwells in me." Romans 7:14-20

Allow me to give you my summary of what Paul is trying to express. Read the following and then go back to the scripture and see if it makes rational sense. Please take your time with the scripture and let the Holy Spirit make this passage real. I labor at this point because I have listened to both pastors and church members use this passage as proof text for continuing in sin. Don't use such passages as an excuse for laziness! If God did not intend for you to overcome the faults and failures in your life He would be found in contradiction. For Him to command us to go and sin no more and then give us a rationalization for continuing to sin goes against His nature.

Here is my summary: 'I want to be all that I can be in this life, yet there is this weight that drags me down. This weight lives within me every single moment of my life. It is a constant pain that nags at my conscious mind as an accuser and stimulates my subconscious mind to the extent that before I know it I am committing a sin that I have confessed dozens of times, swore never to do again and yet I find myself within its clutches. I know that this is not what God has intended for me;

there must be more. Oh, the anguish of spirit I experience daily. How have I dealt with this impossible and crippling dilemma, you may ask? Let me tell you. I have come to the conclusion that it is a fact, that no matter how hard I try, regardless of what I do, how often I pray, how much scripture I memorize, all of these things do not change the fact that this weight of doing that which I abhor is now right here with me. And it will abide with me until I leave this fallen flesh. That being the case I refuse to let it defeat me. I will not let it cripple me. I choose to accentuate the righteousness of God in my life. I have come to the understanding that though my flesh may fail me, the spirit of righteousness within me will prevail. I can and will serve this righteousness no matter how much this weight may try to exert its dominance.'

Picture having to hoist a huge sack laden with all the things of your past upon your shoulder and then going through your day never setting it down. If you do this you will grow stronger with each day. The difficulty for most believers is not found in the sack; we all have our own sacks. The difficulty is in refusing to pick it up and move forward. Now picture this bag as being limited in capacity and it must remain full. It can only hold a certain amount. You cannot lighten your load, but you can change the contents. If you are to take out the things you abhor carrying, you must put something in their place. If you wish to remove deceitfulness from your sack, then begin telling the truth; If you dislike the sexual lust that controls your thoughts, then think about your love for your wife. You see, you cannot think of another woman and your wife at the same time without realizing you are violating your marriage. Your sack won't hold the two; one will have to go.

After a while you will realize that you are stronger and because this sack holds things you desire it becomes lighter.

Before long you are no longer exhausted from the drudgery of your life and you begin to notice the sacks of those around you and because you have strength that exceeds your sack you are able to assist others. You cannot carry their sack for them, but you can enable them with encouragement and by providing an example for them to follow. But you must first pick up your sack!

Sound like an oversimplification? Sure it is. But the truth is you cannot begin to change your mind until you decide that no matter how much you may fail you are going forward, even if you have to face the embarrassment of lugging around things that cause your sack to bulge. You are who you are. God knew what He was getting when He chose you before the foundation of the world. And still He sent His son to the cross to redeem your life. Understand this statement: "The only thing you will ever do without fail, is fail!"

Therefore if the only thing you will do without fail is fail then don't worry about it. If failure is assured, stop expending mental energy toward your failures and concentrate on where you succeed. If I lie fifty times a day for most of my life and suddenly I begin to speak the truth in one of those fifty times I must concentrate on the fact that in one situation I spoke the truth. If I do this before long I will change the ratio. And you can find comfort in the fact that truth is a much weightier matter than falsehood, yet its burden is lighter. You keep telling the truth and before you realize it your life is marked by honesty and truthfulness. That's a much easier sack to carry.

"No more prison sentence"

The primary tool the adversary uses to keep us burdened by our failures is guilt. In my own life the guilt of all I had done against God kept coming to mind continually. I would try to pray and either expend all my effort groveling for acceptance into God's presence so He might hear me or start thinking of a past incident and simply give up because I was so unworthy and unfit to be in His presence. Fortunately for us, Paul did not stop this discourse with the last verse in chapter seven.

"There is therefore now no condemnation for those who are in Christ Jesus." Romans 8:1

I was studying this verse one day when I discovered something about the word 'condemnation'. What I discovered became the single most liberating experience of my Christian existence. The realization of forgiveness I experienced the moment I surrendered to the cross as a young man compares in intensity. However that original burst of joy didn't last because of all the habits and vices that filled my sack. Here is what I discovered: this word literally means, 'penal servitude' or 'prison sentence'. I thought about this for a few moments and then coupled what Paul was saying in the last of chapter seven with the meaning of this statement.

I had always pictured myself sitting in the prison cell of guilt and condemnation when Christ unlocked the door and called me out. I came out with jubilation only to commit a sin and remember I was a sinner, so I turned around and walked back into the cell. Satan closed the door behind me and I watched him go through the motion of locking it. With this truth now in mind I realized that he was only going through the motions. I understood that when Christ unlocked the door to this prison of condemnation he destroyed the mechanism in the lock. If I stayed in this prison it was by ignorance or choice. At that very moment I got up from the bed of self-condemnation and pity and bolted out of that cell to freedom. From that moment on I have lived with the fact that if Christ doesn't condemn me I cannot justify condemning myself.

Even though I have this 'body of death' abiding with me (as Paul calls the co-existence of sin in the flesh of the born again child of God), I do not have to live in the prison of guilt. That sounds as if I am accepting being a double-minded man (James commands us to stop being such). It appears that I am promoting hypocrisy. After all, if I fail in my walk as a believer and yet keep moving forward as if the faults don't matter will I not appear to be faking it? Perhaps, but if you keep living in guilt, sitting in your prison cell, you will never escape the environment of blame and move into the realm of liberty. It is only in the realm of liberty that you can grow.

When I walked out of that cell realizing it would never again be my home, it changed my prayer life. I ceased spending all my prayer time groveling for acceptance. Instead I began to picture myself coming into the throne room of God, bowing in reverence and respect, then standing up worthy to stand before a righteous God boldly making my petitions. There are those who object to such an image. They contend that God will not allow sin into His presence. I remember early in my walk I was instructed to keep a 'sin list'. This list was to be a tallying of all my failures that I would then take into my prayer closet and confess. Then after I had gone through the list I could begin to make petitions before God. If God then failed to answer my prayers it meant that my list was incomplete. If I expected to ever get anywhere I needed to spend more time searching out my failures and confessing them. The only thing this made me want to do was give up.

You may respond with, "But isn't the purpose of Lake Mind to help get rid of those things that cause you to continue in sin?" Yes, the distinction is that Lake Mind is a process that allows the Spirit of God to perform cleansing by replacing sinfulness with righteousness. Keeping a list is a continual wallowing in our failures. It is the role of the Spirit to convict us of righteousness.

Examine the following teaching Christ gave concerning the work of the Holy Spirit. *"Nevertheless I tell you the truth. It is to your advantage that I go away; for if I do not go away, the Helper will not come to you; but if I depart, I will send Him to you. And when He has come, He will convict the world of sin, and of righteousness, and of judgment; of sin, because they do not believe in me; of righteousness, because I go to my Father and you see me no more; of judgment, because the ruler of this world is judged.* John 16:8-11

This passage defines the role of the Spirit in our lives. First He is called to replace the physical presence of Jesus. As I examine the gospels I find the disciples getting into difficulties only when they are away from the Lord's presence. Much like me as a child, they behave when they knew He was looking at them. My dad used to threaten me with, "Don't let me catch you doing _____." So, I would make sure he wasn't around whenever I finished that statement with my actions.

The understanding we have is this: when Jesus was physically here on the earth He was limited by time and space. now that He has ascended and sent the Holy Spirit in His place, He is unlimited and can be in all places at all times. Now He is meeting the needs of all believers in the world, not just a few in an isolated location. Therefore we conclude that no matter where we are, we are in the presence of our Lord. That is why as believers we cannot ever escape the conviction of the Spirit. While we cannot escape His convicting role in our life we do often confuse it. His work in being the convicting representative of Jesus is threefold.

His first work is to convict the lost of their sin. Their unbelief in Jesus causes their minds to know their sin and sinfulness. I believe this is one reason a lost man will sin all the more once he moves in a particular direction. Were it not for the institution of government that God has ordained to control unrighteousness we would annihilate man from the face of the earth with our degradation. Apart from this convicting work a man cannot be converted. This is why you may hear preachers proclaim that we must get a man lost before he can be saved.

The second aspect of His convicting work is toward the believer and the nature of this convicting work is righteousness. Once we are born again, the Spirit begins to focus our attention toward the good we should be doing. It isn't that He ignores our sinful actions, but rather that He draws our attention past such actions to replace them with acts of righteousness. It isn't until we are converted that we are capable of moving past our sin into righteousness.

Finally, He is here to remind us that the enemy has been judged. This is a convicting work in our minds to help us remember the outcome of the battle. When all appears lost, He helps us to know that it is only a façade; we win because Christ has already won!

The Spirit is not the only source of conviction in our mind. We have our own conscience and the accusations of the devil. The above passage helps us distinguish between the conviction of the Spirit and the accusations of the devil. I have found that the devil points out the sinful deed and blames me while the Spirit will point out the sin and then convict me of doing the right thing. For example, I may say something that is not true. The devil will cry, "You are a liar!" The Spirit, however, will begin to urge me to tell the truth and correct the deception.

Remember the distinction made earlier between things that are true and the truth? While it is true that I wrestle with sin, the truth is I have been forgiven, declared righteous by the voice of God, marked with the seal of the Holy Spirit (a reference to a seal made on documents with the kings signet ring), and clothed in the robes of righteousness by the king of kings Himself.

In conclusion, I exhort you to walk toward Him. If you are presently unable to overcome a habit or vice that has been defeating you, ignore it if you must in order to walk toward Him. I assure you it will not be long before you discover how to overcome it.

"It is a forensic declaration"

I want to make one more point before we move on. It has to do with the nature of our standing before God. I call it the 'forensic declaration' of our righteousness. Examine the following passage from Paul's letter to the church at Rome:

"What then shall we say that Abraham our father has found according to the flesh? For if Abraham was justified by works, he has something to boast about, but not before God. For what does the Scripture say? Abraham believed God and it was accounted to Him for righteousness." Romans4:1-4

In the first three chapters of this letter Paul proves unequivocally that all men are lost and deserving of death and hell. His conclusion in chapter three sums it up this way:

"There is none righteous, no not one; There is none who understands; There is none who seeks after God. vs.10&11

And then to make sure he's understood: *"for all have sinned and fall short of the glory of God," v. 23*

He discounts all boasting concerning man's being made righteous and confirms that it is the work of God. (see 3:27-31)

A vast sum of the argument set forth in these three chapters deals with the former estate of the people of God, the Jews, and their dependency on their lineage for assurance of acceptance before God. Therefore he goes to the beginning of their pride (The Jews always boasted that they were the children of Abraham) and lays out the way of righteousness letting them know that salvation has always come by faith.

Paul's statement in verse 4 declares that Abraham believed God and this faith resulted in righteousness. But just what is this righteousness? Is it actual righteousness in that the person is now completely void of its opposite of unrighteousness? Or is it some kind of magic where we really are unrighteous and we are perceived in heaven to be as if we are righteous?

I remember an evangelist coming to our church when I was a young Christian. This gentleman used some different colors of glass and with the right combination he was able to make a black object appear red and then white proving his point that, "When God looks at us through the blood of Jesus we appear pure as snow!" I'm sorry, but that just didn't do it for me.

The key to solving this dilemma is found in the word 'accounted' in verse four. Other translations have this word translated as 'imputed or reckoned'. Regardless of which one you settle on, it is a bookkeeping term that literally means to "Write it down in the ledger".

Understanding this, we realize that what takes place is a legal transaction; it is a forensic declaration. The word forensic means the declaration is legal in nature. Thus Paul is informing us that when God sees our faith in response to the gospel of His son, He opens His book of life and writes next to our name, *Righteous!* The God who spoke this world into existence declares us righteous and just in case you didn't catch it, he makes a written record. Therefore just for the record, I am righteous. And if you have believed and trusted so are you!

Say it to yourself. "I am righteous!" Say it out loud. I challenge you to do it. You might find it habit forming. Also, if you start declaring yourself to be righteous and you catch yourself acting in unrighteous ways, one of two things will happen. First you will be embarrassed that your actions are making you appear to be a phony and you will deal with your sin. Righteousness and unrighteousness are opposites; they cannot co-exist together for very long. Or, you will go the other way and simply give up and quit declaring your righteousness and conclude that you're just a sinner, destined to continue in sin as long as you are in the flesh.

Which way will you go? Come on and give it a try. What have you got to lose except a life destined for failure and defeat?

In conclusion, we are actually, literally righteous even though we may continue to wrestle with sin. A righteous act does not make us righteous, nor does a sin remove that which God has declared and written down. God does not lie nor is He a deceiver.

I'd like to conclude this portion with an illustration. Let's say we are watching an episode of 'Law and Order' on the television. We are watching when Lenny our favorite detective discovers who the culprit is and he arrests him. The program flashes back to the scene of the crime and we actually witness this man commit murder. Then, flashing back to the time of the arrest we detect that something is wrong. Lenny fails to read the prisoner his rights in accordance with the Miranda Act. The scene moves forward to the trial. All the players are here…the attorneys, the judge and jury, the defendant, and the victim's family. Then just as the proceedings begin the defense counsel makes a motion for dismissal of all charges because his client's rights were violated. There are heated exchanges between the attorneys until the judge calls our detective forward and asks him if he failed to read the prisoner his rights. Lenny hangs his head in shame and admits that he simply forgot. In response, the judge declares the defendant acquitted of all charges, bangs his gavel, and tells the guilty murderer he is free to go, never to be charged with this crime.

The victim's family cries out that it is not fair; their family member is gone and this man who is guilty goes free. Some vow revenge and declare their intent to even the score. The judge warns them that to do so would cause their imprisonment. So the guilty walks out of the courtroom a free man. Not an innocent man, but a man acquitted of crime he committed. All based on the declaration of the judge who acts in accordance with the law.

Likewise, you and I are guilty of sin against God and yet the lawmaker of the universe has written a decree that all who trust in His son shall be forever forgiven of all transgressions. And those who have exercised their will in accordance with this decree are right with God and are free from the prison of guilt and condemnation.

APPENDIX
PRAYER

The prayers presented here are based on the following scriptures. I recommend that you spend time reading the Psalms, Ephesians, and Romans for the purpose of cleansing the mind. I also recommend that you use a modern language bible such as the Phillips or Williams translations or The Message by Eugene Peterson. Depending on the time you are able to set aside I recommend that you stick with the Psalms that address your state of mind and repeat them often enough so that they become apart of your idle time thinking. Personalize them by inserting personal pronouns where applicable. At first read the two epistles until they become familiar in theme before you switch to a regular version of the bible for study. Remember it is His word that God uses for cleansing and for speaking to you. I have found that doing something that is automatic following a time reflecting on the word frees up the mind to hear from the Lord. Chores like cutting the grass, riding a bike, or working out on an exercise machine have been the places I have heard from the Lord on a regular basis.

Be patient and give yourself time. Growth is measured best over an extended period of time. If you are just beginning, find someplace private and record your present struggles and the degree to which they plague you and after a few months pull the record back out and see how much difference the word has made. Success begets success so get started and keep it up.

Ephesians 1: 3,15-19

Father,

I come into your presence with praise and thanksgiving. I worship you and acknowledge that you are the Lord of my life and purchased me through the blood of Jesus Christ and I am therefore your property and you may do with me as you will.

You spoke good things about me before You made the world and I agree with all that You said about me and Your word promises that when any two agree on any given thing and they ask for it, they have it. I also agree with you that certain things in my life are in disagreement with what You have said about me and I request Your assistance in their removal.

I ask for a spirit of wisdom and revelation concerning your son so that I will be able to experience the hope of your calling in my life, the riches of Your inheritance, and the greatness of Your power toward me as I believe.

I want to know Your call as a husband/wife of ____________ and realize what it is that You have placed in me that will give me the provision to meet my mate's need in life. Also I want You to enable me to take Your provision, apply it to Your call, and perform in the role that best shows what You spoke about me before the world began.

Fill in your mate's name and then your children, parents, workmates etc.

Outline of chapter one:

I. The eternal plan of salvation for the ages displaying the role performed by both the Trinity and man. Ephesians 1:3-23

A. The Father's plan for our salvation vs. 3-6

B. The Son's provision for our salvation 7-12

C. Man's acceptance, faith and reception of the plan resulting in salvation v. 13a

D. The Holy Spirit takes the plan, the provision, our willingness and belief and

secures us with the seal of ownership by God and begins our transformation as God's possession. Vs.13a & 14

II. Paul prays for these new possessions of God (and us) with application of the totality of the plan of salvation.

A. The prayer begins with a request for an expanded and enlightened mind and Attitude. 1: 15-17

1. The response of faith to the gospel draws Paul's constant prayers vs. 15 &16

2. His request is that we will receive a spirit (attitude) of wisdom (a right use of the knowledge we possess) and revelation (information not yet in our possession) concerning all that is knowable about Christ. V. 17

B. We are in need of this wisdom and revelation in order to experience (*epignosko* the word for full and experiential knowledge) three aspects of our salvation as they correlate to the trinity's work vs. 19-23

1. We are to experience the hope of His calling; (Term for *calling* is same root word found in verse 3 *blessed*; a reference to all that the Father spoke concerning us before the creation of the world.) This is our <u>position</u> in God's plan. When praying for your calling you are praying for your position (note that it is His calling) in the Father's plan, which will always begin where you are in life. Ex. Student, worker, mate, parent, child, citizen, church member and so forth. You are asking the question, "Who am I in the scheme of things in which I have been placed?" v.18 a

2. Next we are to experience the riches of his inheritance; an inheritance is what we <u>possess</u>; (vs. 6-12) we are determined to possess the heritage of God through the fact that we have

been the recipients of so great a salvation. It cost God to possess us and He therefore has an investment placed in us. This part of experience we are to partake in has to do with our value to God. You are asking the question, "Because of the work of Christ who is in me, how do I show the value of the work of God in my life's calling?" (at home, work, school et.) v. 18b

3. Finally we are to experience the resurrection power of God toward us. This is the **potential** of our salvation. The work of the Spirit becomes exhibited in us as a mark of God's ownership and guarantee that what He started He will finish (13-15). This asks the question, "What am I to do with this call and inheritance I have been so freely and undeservedly given?"

4. This power that is ours has been displayed to all realms (physical and spiritual) and all times and has its revelation in the **person** of Jesus Christ. Because of this display all creatures are in subjection to Him and because we are in Him and He is in us. All creation is under our authority when we exercise the Father's call, the Son's provision, and the Holy Spirit's active presence as we work through our salvation by faith. Vs. 19b-23